T0079761

BARBECUE

Edible

Series Editor: Andrew F. Smith

EDIBLE is a revolutionary series of books dedicated to food and drink that explores the rich history of cuisine. Each book reveals the global history and culture of one type of food or beverage.

Already published

Apple Erika Janik *Barbecue* Jonathan Deutsch and Megan J. Elias *Beef* Lorna Piatti-Farnell *Beer* Gavin D. Smith *Bread* William Rubel *Cake* Nicola Humble *Caviar* Nichola Fletcher *Champagne* Becky Sue Epstein *Cheese* Andrew Dalby *Chocolate* Sarah Moss and Alexander Badenoch *Cocktails* Joseph M. Carlin *Curry* Colleen Taylor Sen *Dates* Nawal Nasrallah *Eggs* Diane Toops *Game* Paula Young Lee *Gin* Lesley Jacobs Solmonson *Hamburger* Andrew F. Smith *Herbs* Gary Allen *Hot Dog* Bruce Kraig *Ice Cream* Laura B. Weiss *Lemon* Toby Sonneman *Lobster* Elisabeth Townsend *Milk* Hannah Velten *Mushroom* Cynthia D. Bertelsen *Nuts* Ken Albala *Offal* Nina Edwards *Olive* Fabrizia Lanza *Oranges* Clarissa Hyman *Pancake* Ken Albala *Pie* Janet Clarkson *Pineapple* Kaori O' Connor *Pizza* Carol Helstosky *Pork* Katharine M. Rogers *Potato* Andrew F. Smith *Rum* Richard Foss *Salmon* Nicolaas Mink *Sandwich* Bee Wilson *Soup* Janet Clarkson *Spices* Fred Czarra *Tea* Helen Saberi *Whiskey* Kevin R. Kosar *Wine* Marc Millon

Barbecue

A Global History

*Jonathan Deutsch
and Megan J. Elias*

REAKTION BOOKS

Published by Reaktion Books Ltd
33 Great Sutton Street
London EC1V 0DX, UK
www.reaktionbooks.co.uk

First published 2014

Printed and bound in China
by Toppan Printing Co. Ltd

A catalogue record for this book is available
from the British Library

ISBN 978 1 78023 259 1

Contents

Introduction:
Smoke and Meat

Barbecue occurs at the succulent intersection of smoke, seasoning and flesh. It is arguably the simplest form of cookery; no utensils, equipment or special skills are needed to produce *some* barbecue. One needs a fire, meat and some distance between the two. The rest, as a Talmudist would say, is commentary (we recognize the irony of quoting a rabbi in a barbecue book, given that barbecue is so often pork, but Jews barbecue too, as you shall see).

Much of this commentary is at best confusing, and often simply wrong. Even the English word *barbecue* is confusing, rivalling only the f-word for its versatility: it can be an adjective describing a method of cooking or seasoning; a noun describing a food, an event or a cooking contraption; or a verb. It can be spelled or abbreviated as barbecue, barbeque, BBQ, bbq, BB-CUE, bar-b-q or bar-b-cue – but never *barbe à queue*.

Table 1: The versatile and confusing language of the word 'barbecue'

Part of Speech	Definition	Can You Use It In a Sentence?
Noun	Food, usually meat, prepared by slow smoke roasting (barbecuing).	Honey, I have a hankering. Please pick up some *barbecue* on your way home?
Noun	A gathering at which barbecued food is served.	Would you like to come over for a *barbecue* at my house this Saturday?
Noun	A grill or other piece of equipment on which barbecued food is cooked.	The brisket that has been cooking on the *barbecue* should be done soon.
Verb	To cook by slow smoke roasting (barbecuing).	I will *barbecue* these ribs *char siu* style.
Adjective	Something that has been cooked by slow smoke roasting (barbecuing).	In Croatia, my favourite dish was the *barbecue* (or *barbecued*) lamb.
Adjective	Something seasoned with smoke or spices referencing barbecue flavours.	One packet of *barbecue* crisps please.

Adding to this confusion, all of the above uses of the term *barbecue* (so spelled throughout this volume) are correct and common. In addition, there are some improper and unacceptable uses of the term.

Table 2: Improper and inaccurate uses of the word 'barbecue'

Part of Speech	Definition	Can You Use It in a Sentence?
Verb	Cooking by direct grilling (not barbecuing).	Let's *barbecue* some hamburgers for dinner tonight. Properly: let's grill some hamburgers for dinner tonight.
Adjective	Food that has been cooked by direct grilling.	Should we eat at a Korean *barbecue* restaurant tonight, where thin strips of meat are grilled for a few moments at the table? Properly: should we eat at a Korean grilled meat restaurant?

As you have no doubt gathered, 'barbecue' as properly defined, and as used throughout this book, refers to slow smoke roasting. In order to move forward with a working definition, let's examine each part of this term.

First, slow heat. When cooking on a fire or burning embers (coals), one can cook either directly above or below the coals, or indirectly, some distance away. Cooking above or below the coals or fire uses the radiant heat of the fire to quickly brown and cook the food. If the food is cooked above the radiant heat, the method is referred to as 'grilling'; in the u.s. and Canada, cooking below the radiant heat is referred to as 'broiling'. Neither one is barbecuing.

During barbecuing, air conducts the heat to the food, much as oil conducts heat during frying. The primary cooking process in barbecue is not radiation from the flames of the fire, but rather conduction of heat from the hot air surrounding the food, not unlike oven roasting. In some cases the food is placed a small distance away from the coals or fire – for example, in a home grill one may place burning embers on one side of the grill and the food on the opposite side. In other instances the heat source may not even be in the same chamber as the food, and the heat and smoke may have to travel some distance through ducts.

The second part of our definition is smoke, which is an essential flavour – really the *only* essential added flavour – of barbecue. Therefore barbecue, as properly defined, cannot be cooked in the absence of smoke. When cooking solely on wood or charcoal, smokiness naturally occurs. When cooking with propane or electricity, smokiness must be added, most often through the use of wet wood chips or pellets that smoulder as the food cooks. While some barbecue purists would insist that it is impossible to cook real barbecue with the use of any fuel other than wood (some fundamentalists even reject lighter fluid or gas/electric ignition), as long as real wood or charcoal is present to provide smoke (not liquid smoke, a smoke flavouring), we would grant that the food meets the smokiness criterion.

The third part of our definition, roasting, is one of the simplest and most ancient cooking methods. It simply involves surrounding food (often meat) with hot air, whether in an oven, on a spit or in a pit. In contemporary cooking, meats that are roasted are often lean and naturally tender, such as young chicken, beef tenderloin or rack of lamb, and cook over relatively high heat, 175–130°C (350–450°F), for a relatively short period of time. By slow roasting at 90–135°C (200–275°F), with most finding the sweet spot between 110 and 120°C (225–250°F) in the case of barbecue, tough cuts of meat such as pork shoulder, ribs or brisket, or whole animals – lamb, goat and pig – can become tender while remaining moist.

It is common in conventional roasting to season the meat with salt and pepper and other spices and aromatics before cooking. Lean meats are classically larded (encased or wrapped with fats such as caul fat or bacon) or barded (where strips of fat are laced through the meat), though these practices have fallen out of fashion, except in the case of fowl such as turkeys, which are often cooked with bacon strips laid over the breast. Many commonly barbecued cuts, such as pork shoulder, ribs, whole hogs or beef brisket, are naturally fatty, so don't need to undergo this process.

These three delimiting factors, then, 'slow', 'smoke' and 'roasting', give us our definition of barbecue.

I

Barbecue Beginnings

Barbecue is at once an ancient and very basic form of cookery (fire + meat = barbecue, with seasoning and utensils optional) and a high form of culture complete with formal juried competitions and regional variations from Mongolian lamb (*khorhog*), to Fijian pig, to Chinese *char siu*, to u.s. Pacific Northwest salmon.

Barbecue is probably not much younger than the union of fire and meat themselves. Like many of the world's simple but enduring and culturally significant foods – such as pasta, cheese, ices, flatbreads and fermented drinks such as beer and wine – barbecue as an entity probably developed in numerous locations throughout the world rather than originating in an epiphany-instigated epicentre. It seems unlikely that there was one particular place where humans first discovered that tough cuts of game slowly roasted and smoked away from the fire were more tender than those grilled over direct heat, and disseminated this revelation through cultural exchange.

Nevertheless, some historians and barbecue aficionados search for the invention of barbecue as well as the origin of the word. The catchiest (and notably Francophile) explanation for the origin of the term *barbecue* is that it comes from the French *barbe à queue*, meaning 'beard to tail', said to represent

The beasts pictured in the famous cave paintings of Lascaux would probably have been cooked over open fires some 17,000 years ago.

the whole spit roasting of a pig or other animal. Some U.S. barbecue cooks from the eastern Carolinas, for whom cooking a whole hog is de rigueur, take stock in this definition for its implicit endorsement of whole-hog barbecue over separate butts and ribs, as are more typical elsewhere in the South. But the pervasiveness of the *barbe à queue* definition does not make up for its lack of plausibility. Most scholars argue that while the connection between barbecue and the phrase *barbe à queue* is cute and seems logical, it is based solely on the coincidental sounds of the words. The etymological roots of the term are more likely found in the Arawak and later Creole term *barboka* or *barbacoa*, which describes the grill-like assembly of sticks (*coa*) over a fire on which whole fish and meat were slowly grilled over the coals. The Spanish adopted the term as *barbacoa* and the French as *babracot*, after which it evolved into English as 'barbecue' or 'barbeque'. The word *barbacoa* first appears in print in Gonzalo Fernandez de Oviedo's *La historia general y natural de las Indias* (1526), where it is used to describe spit roasting among the native peoples of the Caribbean.

The First Barbecue?

Anthropologists have discovered evidence that early hominids, the ancestors of modern human beings, applied fire to pieces of meat as long as 1.5 million years ago.[1] This evidence was discovered in southern Africa, now home to the braai, a traditionally Afrikaans version of barbecue featuring such local treats as *boerewors*, a circular sausage, and *sosatie*, a South African kebab.

Palaeoanthropologists have recently figured out how to determine just how hot the fires were that burned bones discovered at ancient sites. Because forest fires tend to burn at much lower temperatures than fires kindled for cooking, scholars have been able to determine that some bones (and the animal flesh that surrounded them) found at ancient dwelling sites were cooked intentionally in cooking fires, as opposed to being unfortunate victims of grass or forest fires.[2] While we don't know exactly how the meat was flavoured – for instance, whether it received salting, spicing or any kind of marinade – we do know that these early meats were not boiled in a pot. Thinking about the available technologies, it makes sense to imagine that pieces of meat were held in or very near the fire on a stake or spit of some kind, probably a tree branch; buried in coals; or set alongside the fire to capture radiant heat.

In order to make sure that the branch itself did not combust and the important lump of protein burn up in the fire, the best method would be to use a green, recently cut stick and to keep the stake at some distance from the flames.

Experimentation would also lead to the discovery that keeping meat slightly further from the fire for a longer time produces more tender meat than meat charred directly on the flame – a great advantage for our ancient ancestors, whose teeth were not as sharp as those of carnivores and who were cooking game that had not been bred for tenderness, as modern farmed meat is. Whether these culinarily adventurous hominids were able to rig up some kind of spit and enjoy barbecue before *Homo sapiens* even arrived on the scene is still unknown.

Studying the probable physiological energy needs of northern European Neanderthals, who lived 125,000 years ago, the archaeologist Bent Sørensen has proposed some compelling evidence that a type of barbecue was used during this era. In order to transport the large pieces of meat needed to sustain physical activity from the site of the hunt to their homes, Sørensen argues that Neanderthals must have dried the animals' flesh in order to reduce its bulk. The quickest and most effective method for doing this was fire, producing a kind of woolly mammoth jerky/barbecue that could sustain communities for almost two months. Since anthropologists now argue that human beings who lived outside of Africa mated with Neanderthals, perhaps they learned their barbecue skills, too.[3]

The Spit and the Broil: Barbecue Predecessors

References to spit roasting (which after all can be a type of indirect smoke roasting depending on the distance between fire and spit) in ancient texts give us confidence that the secrets of barbecue have long been known. In Homer's *Odyssey*, the hero Odysseus returns home in disguise after ten years of

Greek pottery image of boys roasting sacrificial meat on a spit, 450–430 BC.

eventful wandering to a meal of barbecue provided by his old servant, Eumaeus. Not recognizing his former master, Eumaeus nonetheless offers the kind of hospitality that Greek tradition prized highly. Noting that it would be wrong to turn a stranger away, and that 'every beggar and stranger is from Zeus', he went straight to the pigpen. Having picked out two suckling pigs, he 'slaughtered and singed them both, then jointed and spitted them', roasting them up as a simple meal for the visitor. Eumaeus invited his old master to dine, saying, 'Eat the food, Stranger, that a servant can provide.' Odysseus 'sprinkled it over with white barley meal' before eating – an

Cook fanning the fire to roast the duck he is holding in his left hand,
Egypt, *c.* 2000 BC.

intriguing avoidance of the mustard-versus-vinegar-versus-tomato-based-sauce debates of modern times.

Studies of Egyptian paintings and texts indicate that in the homes of the wealthy special racks were used to slowly smoke-roast geese and large joints from other animals, such as gazelles. While the meats were roasting, servants waved fans over them to draw up the heat and smoke. The majority of Egyptian images related to cookery, however, show meat being boiled, which seems to have been the most common treatment in the ancient world. Ancient Israelites likewise usually boiled meat as part of a pottage or grain-based stew, perhaps a precusor to the present-day Sabbath *cholent*. For the annual celebration of Passover, however, it was essential to roast a lamb.[4]

Because of their size, lambs were most likely roasted on spits rather than in ovens. The Passover seder, then, might be considered an annual barbecue that recalls the outdoor cookery necessary to the wandering life of the Jews after their liberation from slavery in Egypt. The legendary king Solomon seems to have valued barbecue quite highly. According to tradition, he is the author of the book of Proverbs, which contains the advice, 'The slothful man roasteth not that which he took in hunting: but the substance of a diligent man is precious' (12:27). For his time and place, this was especially good advice. To roast what you had killed was one way of preserving meat for a longer period of time, particularly if the diligent hunter was able to apply lots of smoke and dry the meat in the process, creating a substance that was both precious, in that it could provide for future needs, and also tasty.

For all their sophistication and conquest of distant regions, the Romans seem to have been indifferent to barbecue. While there are Roman recipes for roasted meats, most of the roasting seems to have been done in enclosed

The breyling of their fish ouer the flame of fier.

John White's painting of native Virginians grilling fish, 1585–6, also looks like a variation on planking – the fish are hung on sticks close to a fire.

ovens. Their preference for this method may reflect the fact that cookbooks were produced for an urban elite, and that spit roasting would not have been particularly convenient in densely populated areas. Or it may be that the kind of cuisine Romans enjoyed did not lend itself to slow roasting over open flames or to pit cooking. A recipe for 'plain roasting' from Apicius, the late fourth or early fifth century AD Roman cookbook, instructs readers to 'simply put the meat to be roasted in the oven, generously sprinkled with salt and pepper'. That the meat was later to be served glazed with honey, however, gives this dish a passing resemblance to more modern barbecue. An elaborate recipe for stuffed pig stomach includes an interlude during which the pig's stomach, already boiled after having been stuffed with brains, eggs, nuts and many spices, is hung near – but not in – the smoke of a fire 'to take on colour'. Since this delicacy is then returned to a pot to boil before being served, it does not necessarily fit contemporary definitions of barbecue, but it is nonetheless interesting to see that smoking was a flavouring technique used in Roman kitchens, even if only in combination with other methods.

According to the account of a Greek visitor, Poseidonius, who lived in the first century BC and travelled throughout the Roman Empire, ancient Celts roasted large pieces of meat on spits. The advent of the Iron Age in Europe in the sixth century BC made this a much more practicable way to cook, although one still needed sufficient wealth to afford the heavy metal and the labour to fashion and turn a spit. Although Poseidonius' text has been lost, another Greek writer, Athanaeus, who lived at the end of the second century AD, quotes Poseidonius' observation that Celtic 'food consists of a few loaves, and a good deal of meat brought up floating in water, and roasted on the coals or on spits.' The detail about the meat floating in water perhaps means that the meat had been boiled before being roasted or that it was soaked in brine before roasting. Either way, Poseidonius' account of the consumption of this food – 'they eat their meat . . . like lions, taking up whole joints in both their hands and gnawing them' – should be recognizable to any barbecue lover today.

While Europeans did roast meats over fire in the late Stone Age, by the Middle Ages this activity tended to be reserved for the homes of the very wealthy, as it involved not only specialized equipment but also careful attention from a 'spit boy' whose task was to sit by the spit and turn it. Spit roasting also required the economic wherewithal to afford large pieces of meat. Although expensive and time-consuming, spit roasting was a good option for large gatherings because whole pigs, sheep and calves – and multiple chickens, duck

Francesco del Pedro, etching of a party of gypsies preparing a meal in the open, 1770–1800. In the centre is a cooking pot over an open fire, with a man spearing a chicken on a spit. At the left is a woman plucking a goose next to another holding a barrel.

and geese – could be roasted at the same time if one had a large enough spit.

By the medieval era English cookbooks included references to spit roasting that often included sweet and sour flavourings. These hint at the barbecue sauces that were to develop centuries later in North America. One Robina Napier, writing in the late fifteenth century, provided a recipe for roast heron that involved cleverly tying the bird to the stake with its own flayed skin. While roasting, the bird was to be sauced with a mixture of vinegar, mustard, powdered ginger and salt.[5] The *Good Housewife's Jewell* (1596) by Thomas Dawson suggested spit roasting a kind of meatloaf constructed of slices of cooked meat mixed with egg yolks, raisins, dates and spices. Once the cook had been able to 'work it together' he was to 'put it on a spit, and set platters underneath it, and

Richard Purcell, *The Cook Maid, c.* 1746–66, etching and mezzotint.

baste it with butter, and then make a sauce with Vineger, and ginger, and suger.'

In the sixteenth century the English cookbook author Gervase Markham noted the adoption from the French of a method known as *carbonado*, which he described as 'meat broyled upon the coals'. Before grilling it was essential to 'scotch it both above and below, then sprinkle good store of salt upon it, and baste it all over with sweet butter melted', 'scotching' being a term for scoring the meat. The German cookbook author Franz de Rotzier, in his *Kunstbuch von mancherley Essen* of 1598, agreed that in order to cook a carbonado properly one 'must always beat [pieces of meat] with the back of a knife before they are grilled so that they become tender'. Markham advised using 'a plate iron made with hooks and pricks, on which you may hang the meat, and set it close before the fire, and so the plate heating the meat behind as the fire doth before, it will both the sooner and with more neatness be ready.' While cooking, the meat was to be turned and 'basted it till it be very brown', then served with butter and vinegar.

Cookbooks, archaeological records and the accounts of travellers reveal that by the time Europeans encountered Caribbean barbecue, they had not only developed similar methods for cooking, but had established a culinary connection between roasted meat, pungent vinegar and a variety of spices which became an important part of the North American barbecue tradition. This particular kind of cooking was often also flavoured with male competition. Our next chapter explores the cultures of barbecue that make meat-on-a-spit more than just a (really good) meal.

2

Man and Feast

Regardless of whether we are discussing Hawaiian *kalua* pig, Mongolian boodog, Mexican *barbacoa de cabeza* or a Spanish bull roast, barbecue is considered across many cultures to be a man's domain. It is unclear why this is the case. Much of the literature is quick to point out the machismo of barbecue, but avoids the question of 'why' by substituting clichés and stereotypes for real answers. Consider, for example, an explanation from a barbecue cook himself: 'It's the caveman in us. I think that's why you see more and more men barbecuing. It's a macho thing. Playing with fire and being outdoors, bragging about how good you cook, it's got all the macho rush to it without any of the violence.' This argument neatly forgets the existence of cave women, as well as the long tradition of female involvement in home butchering and the roasting of meat. It reflects a cultural dichotomy between indoor and outdoor space in which the former is coded as female and the latter as male. This is a relatively recent construction that is specific to societies in which industrialization occurred during the nineteenth century.

When household production was replaced with large-scale manufacturing of consumer goods, domestic space in these societies – the United States and England primary among them – took on a new character. Instead of being a place of productive busyness and its concomitant mess, the home (if only in ideology) became a serene sanctuary managed by passionless females. The temple of the home did not include animal sacrifice, and in America barbecue, because it had to be done outdoors, became an exclusively male business. Because it was so often served at political gatherings, also forbidden to 'respectable' ladies of the late nineteenth century, barbecue emitted an even more masculine odour amid the smoke. In the film version of *Gone With the Wind* (1939), set around the time of the U.S. Civil War, Scarlett O'Hara is urged by Mammy, the enslaved woman who dresses her, to eat something before she goes to a local barbecue so that she may maintain her femininity. When Scarlett says 'I will do my eating at the barbecue', Mammy responds, 'Well if you don't care what folks says about this family, I does!' While it had become acceptable in the mid-nineteenth century South for a woman to attend an event at which smoked meat was the centrepiece, it was still taboo for her to tuck in with gusto.

While these new gender norms explain the twentieth-century association of men with outdoor meat cookery, a likely explanation for the older association of men with barbecue is that in most traditional, non-herding societies, men have been hunters, responsible for the animal protein in a community's diet. Because this protein was a sporadic rather than a constant element in the diet, it held a special status. Meat, in other words, was power. Thus the provider of the meat might well have also become its preparer, preserving the connection to the meat that made him important to his community.

In many cases, too, meat has had to be cooked quickly so that it will last for the length of a journey from hunting ground to home. Smoke and drying, as discussed in chapter One, have long proved excellent tools for preservation. In this case, men barbecued meat because men caught meat, and they did so in the company of other men. They might eat their smoked meat with women and children once it had been transported back to a settlement, and preserved meat might be used by women in compound dishes, but the first cooking process was often male. As the American Studies scholar Elizabeth Englehardt writes, 'For many, the symbols of barbecue's masculinity – cowboy imagery, hunting metaphors and unaffected food presentation are indistinguishable from barbecue itself.'[1] Thus to be 'authentic', that most chimerical of edible properties, barbecue has to be masculine.

In ancient Northern Europe, barbecued meats were often reserved for warriors, probably because of the time and fuel commitment they required, or perhaps because they tend to be large pieces of hacked flesh, reminiscent of the battlefield. In the great Irish epic *Bricriu's Feast*, for example, Bricriu attempts to stir up trouble among local kings by secretly promising each the 'champion's portion' at a feast he has prepared for them. The heroes of the land were expected to fight to the death over 'a caldron of full generous wine', a seven-year-old boar raised on a special diet of milk, nuts and broth, and a 'cow-lord full seven-year-old' fed on sweet milk and herbs. Given the sizes of these beasts and Celtic culinary tradition, we can assume that spit roasting rather than stewing would have been the cooking method and the resultant barbecue flavour would thus have been worth risking life and limb for.[2]

In Papua New Guinea barbecue has also been associated with warfare. Among the Iatmul people, when one village engaged in warfare with another, 'the [returning] warrior staged a pig feast inside the cult house in order to evade the wrath of his victim's ghost.' At this feast, the warrior was 'specifically obligated to feed men of other descent groups', rather than his own people, and to abstain from eating any food himself. The ritual served as a kind of rebalancing between men and the powerful spirits believed to manage human affairs. The meal itself would be prepared in the traditional manner, with the pig roasted in a pit lined with banana leaves. Because the pig feast was so closely connected with the masculine role of warfare, modern-day Papuans, generally at peace with their neighbours, stage mock battles in order to justify the meal.[3]

Barbecue was also associated with the less violent competition between men that was the ancient Greek Olympics. As portrayed in illustrations found on ancient vases, athletes roasted meat every day of the Games by holding it on stakes over altar flames. The sacrifice was made in order to win the favour of the gods for the day's events. While the athletes themselves enjoyed the flesh, the gods savoured the essence of barbecue – the smoke. Demigods, too, enjoyed barbecue, although they managed to sink their teeth into the flesh. According to Greek mythology, that most manly of men, Hercules (or Herakles), was once entertained by the centaur Pholos, who 'set before his guest roast meat, though he himself fared on it raw.' When Hercules talked his host into opening some of the special wine of the Centaurs to wash down his barbecue, all hell broke loose; the famous hero had to fight his way out with the use of poisoned arrows, accidentally killing his host in the process.[4]

Victory banquets for Olympic athletes, popular historian of the Games Tony Perrottet explains, 'existed as a domain of male pleasure' at which the only women welcome were prostitutes hired as entertainment. Rules existed concerning how many fingers, and which ones, could be used 'for each type of food and its quantity'. The barbecued meats served at the victory banquets included 'roasted sow's womb . . . veal kebabs . . . and freshly killed boars, stags, and gazelles from the surrounding mountains', which were presumably spit roasted in the traditional Greek style.[5]

In ancient Greece barbecue could soothe men's grief as well as accentuating their joy in victory. When Achilles mourned his friend and fellow soldier Patroclus, other warriors 'feasted them with an abundant funeral banquet'. According to the *Iliad*, 'many a goodly ox, with many a sheep and bleating goat did they butcher and cut up; many a tusked boar, moreover, fat and well-fed did they singe', thereby removing its hair, 'and set to roast in the flames of Vulcan'. To underscore the connections between warfare and barbecue, two male domains in Greek culture, Homer noted in Book XXIII that while these preparations were going on, 'rivulets of blood flowed all around the place where the body was lying'.

Although Westerners have long imagined Hawaiian luau feasts to be the sort of bacchanalia at which inhibitions between men and women can break down, leading to romance, Hawaiian pig feasts were traditionally only attended by men. Before Europeans arrived in the Pacific in significant numbers and began to influence Polynesian cultures, Hawaiians observed food taboos that included gender segregation during meals and a strict prohibition against women eating pork. According to food historian Kaori O'Connor, before Hawaii became a destination for Western tourists in the nineteenth century, 'Hawaiian eating and feasting were part of a culinary culture linked to religion.' Feasts were supposed to feed the gods, not the people, although men performed the actual mastication.[6] Food was first laid in the mouths of large statues of the gods and then eaten by priests and other important men. Although the *kalua* pig and packets of food steamed in ti leaves were no doubt delicious, divine rather than human pleasure was

Hares roasting the hunter! German ornamental engraving, *c.* 1465–1500.

the focus of the feast. Only men were considered important enough to preside over this interaction with the sacred. When Hawaiians adopted Western traditions they set aside some of their food taboos, including the rule that men and women could not eat together. As the native people of the islands adopted Christianity, the need to feed the traditional gods became less vital, but the tradition of pit roasting pigs was clearly too good to give up and the luau became a more secular pleasure, employed to celebrate important events in human lives.

Sometimes barbecue has been an all-male event not for religious reasons but because of gendered divisions of work. The gauchos of South America, for example, men who herd cattle across vast distances, have traditionally been male. While their main employment was always to move cattle from one place to another, that other place sometimes turned out to be their own bellies. In 1863, Francis Ignacio Rickard published his account of a journey across the Andes, telling of one evening when he and his servant ate 'the genuine *asado* of the gaucho' spit roasted near a fire.[7] Rickard offered the standard assessment of barbecue as delectably savage when he announced, 'I must say for a piece of "Gaucho" roast-beef I would most willingly give up the best dish that was ever placed on the *table d'hôte* at the Hôtel du Louvre in Paris.'[8]

In 1912, when the American newspaper man William Dickson Boyce wrote about his travels in Argentina, he expanded on the theme of the gaucho's masculinity. Aside from a simple stew and the *asado*, the gaucho 'knows no other way of cooking', being nearly undomesticated by the standards of Boyce's time.[9] Notable for his endurance of hunger, when the gaucho ate, Boyce claimed, 'he eats inordinately large quantities of meat', exhibiting a lack of delicacy and a love of flesh that Boyce's culture associated with manliness. To put the finishing touches on his portrait of a thoroughly masculine man, Boyce added this colourful touch: 'His sole weapon of offense and defense is the same long knife with which he cuts off his chunk of *asado*.' The reader is left to imagine that the blood of an enemy might serve as the gaucho's barbecue sauce.

Barbecuing as a male activity has a long history in North America. While most food in Native American communities was cooked by women, meat or fish caught at a distance from a village was sometimes smoke-roasted in order to preserve it for the journey home. As the American writer Nelson Algren stated,

> broiling was accomplished by putting meat on the end of
> a pointed stick and holding it over a fire. When the hunter

A member of the Union army Zoave battalion during the U.S. Civil War roasts wild animals for 'extra rations', 1864, chromolithograph.

EXTRA RATION.

cut a smooth stick and thrust it through the body of the bird or animal he had killed, he could rest the two ends of the stick on stones and roast the meat over coals . . . the barbecue was adapted by the white buffalo hunters from the Indian methods of barbecuing.[10]

The American ethnographer George Thornton Emmons, who travelled in the Northwest in the 1880s and '90s, wrote,

I have seen Chilkat hunting parties cook goat meat by putting it in a hole dug under the fire after it had died down. The hole was lined with skunk cabbage leaves and the meat was covered with leaves and ashes. Then hot coals were hauled over the pit and the fire was rebuilt with heavy logs and left until morning.

The technique described is similar to Polynesian pig roasting, but while Polynesian men roasted as a religious rite, the Chilkat men roasted as part of their role as hunters. Performing the traditionally male work of barbecuing can give Native American men a feeling of connection with traditional roles and ancestors. One Tlingit man, plank-baking salmon in modern-day America, noted, 'Every salmon bake I do, I get butterflies . . . To a lot of people, it's another day. To me, this is a ceremony.'[11]

As Algren noted, European settlers in America adapted barbecue to their own social needs, using it to feed large gatherings of people. The raucousness of such events was satirized by the eighteenth-century American playwright Robert Munford in his unpublished drama *The Candidates; or, the Humors of a Virginia Election*. At a campaign barbecue three characters become so drunk that two – a man and a woman to whom he is not married – pass out. The woman's husband plays a cruel trick on his wife and friend by dragging her body on top of the other man's. When she awakes she will assume her virtue has been compromised. Munford seems to be suggesting that the combination of barbecue and politics brings out the worst in people.[12] In the popular book *Fried Green Tomatoes at the Whistle Stop Cafe*, later adapted into a film, author Fannie Flagg offered a twist on this notion. Barbecue is used to dispose of the savagely abusive husband of one of the story's heroines. When the man is found to be missing, a detective arrives at the barbecue restaurant where his wife works, only to enjoy five platefuls of the man he is attempting to find.

It was not until universal white male suffrage involved all classes of white men in the political process in the U.S. in the 1840s that barbecue began to play a big role in political campaigns. Writing at the end of the nineteenth century, the Methodist preacher Louis Albert Banks recalled the political barbecues of his childhood in Oregon: 'Instead of taking up collection of money for campaign purposes, the political committees would go about through the neighborhood and get donations of fat steers and sheep and hogs.' At the site of the planned barbecue, the animals were butchered and hung up while

> a long trench was dug in which a big fire was kept burning for many hours and about midnight before the day of the meeting the animals were put whole in this trench over the glowing coals. They were skewered with long green poles, and very carefully looked after for about twelve hours until they were thoroughly cooked.[13]

Not only the collection of money but the care taken over the meat would have been men's work, since women were commonly assumed to be in danger of corruption if they handled money or lingered too long in public at night. In Southern communities African American men usually performed the work of cooking at large public barbecues. In a story by Arthur Firmin Jack about a political barbecue in Georgia at the end of the nineteenth century, 'Negroes, stationed at the pits, were busily occupied and sweating, in basting the carcasses, which work had been proceeding slowly, constantly, and carefully for many hours, as it must be up to standard 'cue quality.' Thus while barbecue was a source of pride for whites – Jack notes that 'Georgia is the state for 'cues (though a Kentuckian will tell you differently)' – it was often the work of African Americans, who used the relatively high value placed on this work to earn money by establishing their own

The Grand Army of the Republic veterans' barbecue, *c.* 1895, stereopticon slide.

eating places. Southern chef Jason Sheehan claims, 'There were dining rooms, backyards, and roadhouse juke joints in the South that were integrated long before any other public places.' On the other hand, some barbecue joints remained segregated even after civil rights legislation made this illegal. While a barbecue joint could unite people in pleasure, it could also be a battleground.[14]

In Zora Neale Hurston's famous novel *Their Eyes Were Watching God* (1937), the residents of an all-black town in Florida prepare a barbecue to celebrate their greatest moment of civic achievement when the first lamp post is lighted on a public street. Considering what will be appropriate to the occasion, the mayor declares, ''Tain't nothing people lak better 'n barbecue. Ah'll give one whole hawg mah ownself.' The women of town are asked to make the pies and 'That's the way it went, too. The women got together the sweets and the men looked after the meats.' When the lamp was finally lit, the crowd sang a hymn, 'over and over until it was wrung dry . . . Then they hushed and ate barbecue.' The implications of barbecue's divinity are clear – it is the first thing you put into a mouth made holy by singing hymns.

The food historian Andrew Warnes argues that barbecue's reputation as the opposite of refinement actually made it an attractive food for political campaigns, especially in the case of Andrew Jackson, one of the first presidential candidates to benefit from expanded suffrage. Warnes writes, 'White Americans grasped that there was in Jackson's harnessing of the campaign barbecue a declaration that his was the "savage" ticket, the "cannibal" ticket that could be set against the urbane refinements of John Quincy Adams.' While all politicians might offer campaign barbecues, Warne suggests, only Jackson embodied the technique's masculinity.[15]

One historian describes the entire political process of late nineteenth-century America as 'the Great Barbecue'. Vernon Parrington asks, 'to a frontier people what was more democratic than a barbecue [?]' But this seemingly egalitarian feast, Parrington argued, was functionally unfair, as 'the waiters saw to it that the choicest portions were served to favored guests', while others less influential were served

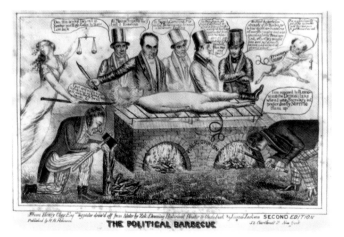

Political cartoon featuring a brick barbecue with a politician (Andrew Jackson) on the grill, 1834.

only scraps.[16] Unfortunately for barbecue fans, the era has generally been known by the less culinary term invented by Parrington's contemporary Mark Twain – the Gilded Age.

Some American politicians became so attached to campaign barbecues that they continued to throw them even after they were elected. Lyndon B. Johnson notably used barbecues throughout his political career to draw people close to him. The historian Hal Rothman notes that 'During his years as senator and vice-president, Johnson had used barbecues to accent his regional identity' as a Texan who could claim both Southern and Western connections.[17] His first state dinner was in fact a barbecue in Texas, to which he invited the West German Chancellor Ludwig Erhard. Rather than manning the grill himself, Johnson relied on the talents of renowned pit master Walter Jetton, who favoured an above-ground pit constructed from building blocks and topped with a mesh grill. Although she spent little time at the grill or in the kitchen, Johnson's wife 'Lady Bird' freely shared her recipe for barbecue sauce, which included butter, catsup, lemon juice, Worcestershire sauce and vinegar.

For the Johnsons, barbecue was much more than a way to feed large crowds. It helped to differentiate them from the distinctly high-culture style of the Kennedys, who had preceded them in the White House. It also allowed Johnson to lend a mood of informality to what were ordinarily stuffy events. This unique kind of power play, slow-smoked and tangy, was dubbed 'barbecue diplomacy' by a reporter for the *New York Herald-Tribune*.

Rothman recounts that Johnson once threw an impromptu barbecue for the travelling press corps, who at the time were predominantly male, at his home in Texas. The invitation read: 'In view of the poor physical condition of the Fourth Estate, the President and Mrs Johnson invite the travelling press to a

President Lyndon Johnson and Hubert Humphrey at a barbecue, 1964.

barbecue.' Reflecting on their itinerant, anti-domestic lifestyles, the invitation reflected common assumptions both about men's inability to feed themselves, and about the appropriateness of barbecue for such a nomadic pack.[18]

Texans celebrated another semi-nomadic pack in 1962 when a giant indoor barbecue was held to honour the astronauts of the NASA's Project Mercury mission. Perhaps the event was meant to connect astronauts to the Texan history of the cowboy, who also journeyed far from home into uninhabited places, or perhaps it was just the *sine qua non* of Texas hospitality. In a memorable scene from *The Right Stuff* (1979), Tom Wolfe recounts how ten barbecue pits had been dug in the Sam Houston Coliseum to feed the 5,000 people attending the event: 'Great cow carcasses sizzled and popped and the smoke of the burning meat was wafted here and there in the chilly currents of the air conditioning. Only the extreme cold kept you from throwing up.' For Wolfe, this kind of barbecue represented American excess rather than nature's bounty or frontier spirit.[19]

As food historian Charles Perry recounts, southern Californians also have a history of making barbecues big events. Adopting and adapting a Mexican tradition, late nineteenth- and early twentieth-century Angelenos threw bulls' head barbecue breakfasts. Various meats were served at these, but a steer's head was the main attraction. According to Perry, the events represented an attempt on the part of white Angelenos to invent traditions for themselves in the region by recreating the feasting style of the first Spanish settlers of the area. Perry posits that interest in these mass events waned as Los Angeles developed a culture more focused on movies and their stars than on reliving the Mexican/Spanish past of the region.[20]

M.F.K. Fisher, one of America's most famous food writers, recalled attending a barbecue in her Southern California

Making barbecue sandwiches at the free barbecue on Labor Day, Ridgway, Colorado, 1940.

A 1950s edition of the *Big Boy Barbecue Book*.

Men eating barbecue in Pie Town, New Mexico, 1940.

youth that strove, like those Perry describes, to recreate a mythologized Spanish past. She was

> taken to a big barbecue . . . to benefit something like the new Elks Club. It was the most authentic I have gone to, I think, in real, early-California style, with long board tables . . . and a big pit where two whole steers had been roasting all night.

The event, she recalled

> would have been all-white, with only the cooks at pitside the real Mexicans. And where was the music? What good

is a real old-fashioned barbecue without at least a couple of guitars and maybe a cornet, to sob it up on 'La Paloma'?[21]

For Fisher, even slow-roasted meat was not sufficient unless flavoured with both traditional music and a spirit of inclusion.

While frequently recognized as keepers of ancient culinary traditions, barbecue chefs are also often portrayed as idiosyncratic in the behaviour they demand of diners. In John Grisham's legal thriller *A Time to Kill* (1989), for instance, customers are given exactly twenty minutes to eat and leave in order to keep business at Claude's, a fictional barbecue restaurant, moving. When reporters for the *New York Times* visit and request chef's salads, the restaurant's owner 'cursed them, and told them to eat barbecue or leave'. In the Kansas City novel *Thin Blue Smoke* (2009) by Doug Worgul, customer choices are similarly limited by an autocratic owner-genius who refuses to serve french fries and insists on keeping his grandmother's recipe for vinegar pie on the menu.[22]

Sometimes decor expresses the quirkiness of a barbecue master. In a loving tribute to Kansas City's famous Arthur Bryant's, Calvin Trillin wrote that the original location 'has no decorations beyond an eye chart', not the obvious choice in restaurant beautification. John Steinbeck wrote of a character who invited large crowds to his farm for a barbecue:

> Raymond was grilling little chickens while a group of admiring men stood about . . . 'If any of you can do it better, step right up,' Raymond shouted at them. 'I'm going to put on the steaks for anyone that's crazy enough not to want chicken.'

Marking the consumer as the outsider seems to be a particular talent of the barbecue chef.[23]

In the u.s. in the late 1940s and '50s the privilege of throwing a barbecue (and making up your own rules about it) suddenly and significantly passed from the exclusive realm of the bankrolled politician to the average Joe. The GI Bill that enabled soldiers returning from the Second World War to buy their own homes had a profound impact on barbecue culture in America, and thus on masculinity. From the early beginnings of the industrial revolution until the postwar era of the 1940s and '50s, middle-class Americans had participated in gender-segregated socialization. Men spent their leisure time with other men and women spent theirs with children or other women. Once military veterans began to be able to buy single-family homes, however, this all changed. Because these homes tended to be in newly built suburbs, at a distance from the traditional male gathering places such as the urban saloon, men found themselves at home more often.

The new ideal in domestic architecture included a large lawn, providing families with a new kind of semi-public domestic space. Guests could be invited over but not into the home, easing the acquisition of more acquaintances without demanding potentially stressful intimacy. The backyard became a space for social engagements where children could play unsupervised and all could relax – the hostess not worried what guests would think of her undusted corners and the guests not worried what the hostess would think of their unpolished manners. To complete the backyard's safely uncivilized atmosphere, barbecue provided a combination of food and entertainment. Men who had been socialized to be uncomfortable in formal gatherings could play at 'savagery' by using flames to cook meat and bare hands to eat it. This trend produced a whole new market for barbecue tools and created a new masculinity for the middle class. The new ideal was a controlled but not disempowered manhood, kept tidily in check from Monday to Friday and let gently loose on the weekends to stand in front of a grill, flipping meat with a spatula.

3
Poles, Holes, Racks and Ovens: The Technology of Barbecue

Barbecue probably has such a long history because it requires so little technology to produce so much flavour. Nonetheless, over time humans have developed tools to help the process along or to adapt it to smaller spaces. This chapter explores the wide range of barbecue tools that have been developed around the world and through the ages. The chapter is organized around the primary methods of barbecuing – poles (spits and stakes), holes (pits), racks and ovens – with the understanding that there is much overlap in methods. Sometimes it takes both spit and pit to do the job well.

Poles

In the famously controversial Peter Greenaway film *The Cook, the Thief, His Wife and Her Lover* (1989), a murdered man is spit roasted and served to his killer as a form of revenge. We prefer barbecue.

One of the least technologically demanding methods of barbecuing uses poles to hold meat at a distance from fire. Spits and stakes hold meats either vertically or horizontally above or next to the fire. It is also common in spit and stake

Pieter Aertsen, *The Cook*, 1559, oil on canvas. Note the spitted birds.

cooking for some kind of rotation to occur. Vertical stakes may be turned upside down at regular intervals and horizontal spits are generally turned. One example of stake barbecuing is the Argentine *asado*, which is practised particularly in the Patagonian region of Argentina. In an *asado* large pieces of meat are pounded flat and tied to cross-shaped stakes – *asadors* – that ring a fire pit. These pits are shallow hollows rather than the deeper trenches used in pit barbecue. In some cases meats are skewered rather than being tied to stakes. This method became more practical once heavier metals were

Samuel De Wilde, *British Cookery or 'Out of the Frying-Pan into the Fire'*, 1811, etching.

introduced after the arrival of Europeans in the Americas: it would, for example, probably be easier to stick a sharpened metal stake through the carcass of a deer than a wooden stake, simply because the metal stake would not be at risk of breaking in the process. Metal skewers would also hold up to the heat of a fire pit better than would wooden poles. And if metal skewers were heated ahead of time, they could work to cook large pieces of meat from the inside. However, wooden stakes seem to have served for hundreds of years to hold meat close to a flame for long periods of time until it was perfectly cooked, and they were certainly easier to transport or cut fresh each time, making it possible to enjoy barbecue while on the hunt for more.

The journalist Bob Shacochis, writing about a visit to Buenos Aires, describes the 'most unusual gastronomic tableau' when *asado* comes indoors, 'behind glass but a campfire

Planked salmon at a salmon cookout.

nonetheless'. Shacochis encountered a restaurant with an indoor fire pit:

> encircling the flames are the sizzling carcasses of perhaps a dozen sheep, each crucified on an *asador* . . . the legs of the animals splayed outward, mounted like grisly butterflies, succulent pennants of roasting flesh, golden and greasy.[1]

Typically *asadors* hold meats perpendicular to the ground but tilted in towards the flame, so that they can benefit from heat without being singed.

Native North Americans became world famous for their barbecuing techniques once Europeans had tasted the results of planking, a common way of cooking salmon in the Pacific Northwest. All kinds of fish and game were cooked using this method, which was similar to the South American *asado*, except that in planking the stakes play more of a role in flavouring the meat. Fish were split and fastened to a wet cedar plank, then placed at a 60-degree angle to a fire. The plank was turned upside down at regular intervals to make sure that the meat cooked evenly. Planking imparts a smoked wood flavour to the food. It became very popular as a method of cooking shad, an Atlantic coast fish, in the nineteenth century, although shad was usually planked on oak rather than cedar. In her famous *Boston Cooking-school Cook Book* (1896), Fannie Farmer offered a recipe for planked shad and noted that 'the Planked Whitefish of the Great Lakes has gained much favor.'[2] In 1915, the cookbook author Edith Thomas was merely repeating what others had been saying for nearly 100 years when she averred, 'After eating planked shad, no one will wish to serve it in any other manner.'[3] Farmer and Thomas, however, both being ladies, baked their planked fish in ovens rather than roasting them around an open fire. They probably also transferred the fish to plates in order to serve it and certainly discouraged eating it with one's hands, the traditional method.

The nineteenth-century essayist Charles Lamb in his *A Dissertation upon Roast Pork* identified the lack of eating utensils as the most important feature in the discovery of barbecue. Long ago in China, Lamb wrote, a dull witted young man named Bo-Bo allowed his father's house to catch fire. All nine of the piglets in the house were burned to death. In trying to remove them from the wreckage, Bo-Bo touched the meat, found it very hot, put his fingers in his mouth to cool them down, and discovered the glory of crackling. If Bo-Bo had used a pitchfork or any other implement to move the carcasses, the story suggests, the world would never have known *char siu*, the world-famous Cantonese barbecued pork.

Lamb's humorous history describes the later introduction of string and spit roasting, which in his version saved the people of China from having constantly to burn down and rebuild their homes for the sake of roast pork. Like the jointed mutton of the traditional *barbacoa*, *char siu* is often cooked in pieces rather than whole, with strips of meat clustered together so that each piece helps to baste the others. Whole ducks, chickens and geese may also be cooked in the same method, which is generally known as *siu mei*. *Siu mei* cooking involves glazing meat with a soy sauce, honey and spice mixture before either hanging the meat on a hook or skewering it. *Siu mei* meats are cooked in very large ovens so that heat gets to all parts of the meat at the same time. In contemporary China the heat for these ovens, which resemble metal smoke houses and are sometimes described as giant rotisseries, comes from charcoal or even gas burners. In the past the fires would have been stoked with wood. To achieve the traditional pink colour once produced by wood smoking, modern *char siu* cooks often resort to the use of red food colouring. Because the equipment required to cook in this

Thomas Bewick, engraving of a monkey roasting a chicken on a vertical spit, *c.* 1800.

style is beyond most families' means and lacks practicality for everyday use, *char siu* and other meats prepared in this style are generally take-out food. *Siu mei* shops all over the world display their shining wares in large windows. *Char siu* pork is often used as the stuffing for soft buns that serve as snacks and provide a cheaper way to enjoy the treat. The American equivalent is the pulled pork sandwich, also a pile of smoked pig, usually with tangy and sweet sauce, served on, rather than in, a soft roll.

Like Chinese meat roasting, European barbecue often took place indoors. Spit roasting, also known as rotisserie, was a common cooking method in large and affluent households. Heavy metal spits were set up in huge open fireplaces and spit boys were employed to turn them. Any juices that dripped into a waiting pan were used to baste the meat. Spits could be horizontal or vertical, making it possible to roast several different kinds of meat simultaneously in one fireplace. A fifteenth-century author of a book detailing the requirements of a prince's kitchen recommended a stunning supply of spit roasting gear:

> Twenty rotisseries, with turning mechanisms and irons for holding the spits. And one should definitely not trust wooden spits, because they will rot and you could lose all your meat, but you should have one hundred and twenty iron spits which are strong and are thirteen feet in length; and there should be other spits, three dozen which are of the aforesaid length but not so thick, to roast poultry, little piglets, and river fowl.[4]

This writer, known as Maistre Chiquart, gave directions for a bit of barbecue hijinks that hosts (with the help of their cooks) might enjoy: 'take a large fat goose, and spit it well and put it to roast and . . . recloth it in the plumage of the peacock and put it in the place where the peacock should be set.'[5] The peacock, too, would be spit roasted, but not served in his usual place and not dressed in his usual feathers. Rotisserie has since become somewhat less elaborate, as electric heat sources have made it possible for individual families to roast whole chickens at home. Commercially produced rotisserie chicken is popular and widely available in many parts of the world. Its advantage over that produced at home is that the many chickens that are roasted together baste each other. In some American barbecue restaurants large wood-fired rotisserie ovens are used to roast a variety of meats together, taking advantage of gravity to keep them basted with a rich variety of juices.

Holes

Another simple method requiring little in the way of specialized tools is the pit roast, as practised by Polynesians for many centuries. This is the style of cooking featured in luaus, those famous feasts popularized internationally in the 1950s by the American restaurateur Victor Bergeron Jr, better known as 'Trader Vic'. Pit cooking uses a controllable fire and means that cooks and their friends do not have to be so close to the intense heat of the flame – an especially important advantage in the warm climates where this style predominates.

In an article in *Boy's Life* magazine in 1949, the writer James English portrayed a luau from a mainland American's perspective. English described the digging of an *imu* pit 'large enough to hold easily the entire pig we were to *kalua*'. *Imu* is the Hawaiian word for an underground oven or cooking pit, and *kalua* the traditional term for cooking in an *imu*. Once the pit had been dug, 'a hot fire of coconut husks and algaroba wood' was kindled under a layer of volcanic rocks. Once the fire had heated the rocks sufficiently, coals were removed from the pit. The pig was then 'slit inside the legs and under the jaw' and 'these slits were filled with 'Hawaiian salt [coarse rock salt] and then hot rocks from the fire were placed inside the pig'. Using the preheated rocks as a cooking tool, Hawaiians were able to cook the pig from the inside out as well as from the outside in.

Leaves of the native ti plant, which are broad and strong, were used to tie the legs of the pig together. The luau that James English attended used some modern Western technology to ease the lowering and lifting of the pig into and out of the pit. Once tied, 'the pig was placed on a matting of banana and ti leaves which covered a piece of chicken wire'. Before chicken wire became available, however, Hawaiians simply used long poles to lower and lift pigs from the *imu*. The purpose of setting the pig on the leaves, English noted, was 'to keep the pig off the hot rocks and also to provide moisture' so that the meat neither burned nor dried out. Too wise to waste such a useful source of heat, Hawaiian cooks traditionally placed other kinds of food in the pit with the pig, wrapped in ti leaf packets. Here the ti leaves acted as steamers, much like the parchment paper packets used in contemporary home cooking.

Once all the food to be cooked had been placed in the pit, 'burlap sacks' – or in the old days, just more leaves – 'were placed over the chicken wire both to keep the heat in and to keep the dirt out' before the pit was refilled. A careful check of the site to make sure that no smoke was escaping was all that was needed. 'Once this was done no more heed need be paid to our dinner for a couple of hours.'[6]

In describing luaus mainland Americans always noted the lack of utensils used in eating the many kinds of food supplied.

For some, like James English, this was a treat: 'It's hard to beat fingers for utensils. They work wonderfully well, and seldom is there a slip between table and mouth.' For others, like the tourist depicted by Blanche Howard Wenner in a comic poem, the experience was disturbing: 'What! Dip my fingers in this bowl of poi!/My appetite is gone – I wonder why.'[7] For native Hawaiians, of course, the traditional technology of fingers and ti leaf plates worked perfectly for enjoying the delectable *kalua* pig and its various leaf-wrapped and roasted side dishes.

Central American and Caribbean cooks have been using technology similar to the *kalua* for their *barbacoa* since long before Europeans arrived in the area. In 1887, nearly 400 years after the arrival of Columbus in the Caribbean, the American travel writer Fanny Chambers Gooch Iglehart wrote in praise of *barbacoa*. Iglehart, who lived in Mexico for seven years, wrote that it was 'one of the principal articles of food known to the Mexican market' and was 'good enough for the table of a king'. To create this royal dish, 'The dextrous native takes a well-dressed mutton, properly quartered, using also head and bones. A hole is built in the ground and a fire built in it. Stone slabs are thrown in, and the hole is covered. When thoroughly hot, a lining is made of maguey leaves' – the long, sturdy leaves of the agave, also known as the century plant. Then, 'the meat put in, and covered with maguey, the top of the hole is also covered and the cooking goes on all night'.[8]

On the next morning the hole was reopened, and 'delicious hot barbecued mutton' could be enjoyed. Iglehart noted that because this cooking technique required a large amount of space, it was not generally practised in private homes. Instead families bought their *barbacoa* at public markets. The luau, too, because it required a lot of outdoor space, heavy rocks and more than one person to lift the pig, was a public meal: it was made to serve large numbers out of doors. The technology of production in the case of both *kalua* and *barbacoa* affected how and where these foods were consumed and what kind of role they played in local foodways. *Kalua* was feast food, while *barbacoa* was produced regularly for public markets.

Atlantic coast Native Americans appear also to have practised pit barbecuing, as archeological evidence collected in the early nineteenth century revealed. Gerard Fowke, working on behalf of the u.s. Bureau of Ethnology, located 'more than 20 barbecue holes' in his investigations of the Potomac region. The holes had clearly been used for barbecue, as the bottoms were 'much burned' and 'in one was a quantity of burned stones.' The pits, which were circular in shape and twice as wide at the top as at the bottom, also contained charcoal, animal bones and mussel shells.[9] The existence of two primary barbecue technologies – pit and grill – continues to characterize North American barbecue, although pit barbecue is almost exclusively associated with the South.

Until the mid-twentieth century North Americans tended to enjoy barbecue at large outdoor gatherings. Traditionally barbecue had been a public event, paid for by political candidates or by the community at large. John Duncan, a Scottish traveller, who visited America between 1818 and 1819, described a Virginia barbecue to which he was invited by a relative of George Washington. Not far from Mount Vernon, in a 'little Glen . . . black men, women, and children were busied with various processes of sylvan cookery.' Duncan gave a good picture of just how much work was involved in preparing the food for a Southern barbecue. The elite members of Southern society were renowned for their hospitality, which was made possible by the large teams of enslaved workers who were skilled in many facets of cooking and entertaining. Duncan observed, 'One was preparing a fowl for the spit, another feeding a crackling fire which curled up round a large pot, others were broiling pigs, lamb, and venison over little square pits filled with the red embers of hickory wood.' The pits, Duncan indicated, were where the really important work was happening: 'The meat to be *barbecued* is split open and pierced with two long slender rods, upon which it is suspended across the mouth of the pits and turned from side to side till it is thoroughly broiled.' At a distance from the pits, an outdoor dining table and dance floor were occupied by the white guests of the event. Duncan noted that local politics were the main topic of conversation among those who did not dance.[10]

A similar process to that witnessed by Duncan is found in North Africa. Moroccan cooks prepare lamb in a method known as *mechoui* that involves two kinds of barbecue technology, both spit and pit. As the cookbook author Fatema Hal describes the method,

> a large hole is dug in the ground, a wooden fire is lit in the hole, and cooks wait for embers to form. The whole lamb is threaded onto a spit and balanced on forked poles that have been placed on either side of the pit. The lamb is then cooked for about six hours.

Hal notes that those without the space to perform this ritual could borrow the use of an oven from the village baker.[11]

Racks

Late sixteenth-century images produced by the English explorer John White in the Outer Banks region of what is now North Carolina reveal that native people of the region barbecued fish by constructing a wooden rack and lighting a

Split barbecue meat at a Lower East Side street fair, New York, *c.* 2008.

fire underneath it. The fish were held a good distance above the fire to keep them out of direct heat. White annotated his watercolour painting to identify the process as 'broyling', an activity familiar to him from English foodways (pictured on p. 20). Although the European introduction of metals to North America offered ways to build more durable grills, the mobile lifestyle of many Native American groups who regularly relocated within a known region probably made the continued use of wooden tools for barbecue more practical.

East Africans have a long tradition of grilling meat over fire, and the Maasai culture is today well known for its *nyama choma*. Because the Maasai were herdsmen, the meat of large herbivores was available to them at all times, unlike native North and South Americans, who grilled what they could catch before herding was introduced, with the arrival of European animals such as the goat and sheep.

Ostrich and crocodile, as well as lamb, chicken, pork and beef roasted on spits, are all on the menu at the Carnivore Restaurant in Nairobi.

Maasai barbecue traditionally uses a wooden grill constructed from whatever is available at the chosen site. Because the Maasai's habitat is not forested and they are semi-nomadic, the only available fuel for the fire is scrub, the dry twigs of small bushes. Scrub will not burn for as long as larger pieces of wood, so the Maasai grill their meat in chunks rather than as whole carcasses. Because the necessary fuel would take a long time to gather, *nyama choma* was food for special occasions only. Contemporary urban barbecue in Kenya uses metal racks and wood or charcoal for grilling, making it available at any time.

South African barbecue, known as braai, was introduced by Dutch immigrants in the nineteenth century. According to legend, braai originated in the exodus of Dutch settlers from coastal South Africa, who left because they were opposed to British colonial policies. In their trek across mountains into the interior, Dutch Africans survived on wild game grilled on wooden racks over wood fires. Time has supplied more sturdy equipment, and some now even use gas grills, although traditionalists swear that the braai must use wood in order to be authentic.

Another semi-nomadic group, Mongolians, developed two barbecue methods that could be easily transferred from place to place, *boodog* and *khorhog*. *Boodog* involves taking a gutted goat or marmot, stuffing the cleaned-out interior cavity with hot stones and cooking the whole beast in front of a fire. *Khorhog* evolved from the culinary practices of Mongolian warriors, who used their metal shields to roast large chunks of meat over fires. Hot stones were also placed inside the carcass in this cooking method. Over time, Mongolians began to use metal canisters instead of shields for this type of cooking. In contemporary *khorhog* heated rocks and chunks of meat, along with vegetables and water, are placed inside a metal canister, where they cook for about one hour. The dish widely known as Mongolian barbecue, which involves cooking thin strips of meat at the table, is really a Taiwanese practice. In Japan restaurants named Jingisukans, after Genghis Khan, serve lamb and mutton grilled in metal pans that are supposed to resemble Mongolian warriors' helmets.

Ovens

The historian Felipe Fernández-Armesto notes that 'In essence, the tandoor is a cooking pit, elevated above the ground.'[12] The basic form of the tandoor, whether above or below ground, is an ancient technology. Tandoor-style ovens have been discovered at ancient sites in Iraq that date back to 5000 BC.[13] The sociologist Michael Symons describes this type of oven as 'like a dumpy chimney, with a fire at the bottom, variously fueled with wood, charcoal, or dung-straw cakes. Since the fire is contained, the tannur uses fuel efficiently.'[14] Variations on the theme can be found in kitchens across Central Asia and the Middle East as well as in South Asia. Persians seem to have brought the technology to northern India, where tandoori cooking has become famous. Meat that has been marinated, usually in a mix of yogurt and spices that has distinctly Middle Eastern roots, is lowered into tandoors on stakes that can be shifted around during the cooking process. Bread doughs are simply slapped against the inside walls of the oven where they stick, quickly roast and emerge with a unique smoky flavour. In 1995 the residents of Delhi, India, were shocked to learn that a member of congress, Sushil Shah, had attempted to dispose of the body of his wife, whom he had murdered, by burning her remains in the tandoor of a successful restaurant.

Americans, too, have used ovens for a kind of barbecue. Perhaps because middle-class ladies were not expected to appear at the kind of rowdy public events at which Americans enjoyed barbecue, cookbooks of the early twentieth century sometimes include a peculiar aberration in the form of oven-roasted meat identified as barbecue. In a cookbook of 1913, *Dishes and Beverages of the Old South*, for example, readers are directed to rub the middle cut of a lamb with pepper, paprika, mustard and Tabasco sauce, roast it on a rack in the bottom of a very hot oven and serve it with a sauce made of butter, vinegar, pickles and onion juice. As the author wrote, 'This is as near an approach to a real barbecue, which is cooked over live coals in the bottom of a trench, as a civilized kitchen can supply.'[15]

In the twentieth century an interest in outdoor activities combined with a boom in the building of single-family homes to inspire middle-class Americans to domesticate the barbecue. What had once been a community event became a casual form

Brick backyard barbecues became fashionable during suburbanization in the 1950s.

of socialization for family and friends. An article in *Gourmet* magazine in 1941 offered readers careful instructions on how to build their own backyard barbecue pits and entertain themselves while tending it all night – with a little liquor and a little live guitar music. The Connecticut-based authors reassured their readers that the deep pit they had just dug in their backyard could be used to burn leaves in the autumn, justifying the time and effort if luscious barbecue were not enough.[16]

In the 1940s outdoor ovens built of concrete and brick were something of a craze, and continued to be featured in advertising for other leisure-related products through the 1950s. An article in *Popular Science* in 1936 instructed readers on how to build their own. A brick barbecue oven consisted of a three-walled brick box with a hinged door, a grate on top and a chimney through which the smoke could escape.[17] There was enough interest in building outdoor ovens for the Sunset Publishing Corporation to produce the *Sunset Barbecue Book* in 1945; it covered such daunting topics as 'Build it or Have it Built?' and 'Building With Bricks and Mortar'.[18]

Most Americans, however, could not afford to build a barbecue, and in any case did not have the space to spare for either a brick oven or a pit. A market in movable lightweight barbecues rapidly developed in the post-war years when millions of first-time homeowners with young families, who were moving into newly built suburbs, began to see their homes as places to entertain. One of the earliest models in this market was the Bar-Be-Kettle, which was first advertised in 1948. This contraption, produced by the W. B. Millison Company in Colorado, had a heavy cast-iron cauldron bottom with short legs and two grates inside – one for the coals and the other for the food – and a flat lid.[19] Other similar products were developed, some with shelves extending from the sides of the kettle to provide space for plates and barbecue tools.

In 1952 the Weber Brothers Metal Works introduced the round-topped kettle barbecue that would be a standard feature of American backyards until the popularization of outdoor gas grills at the end of the twentieth century. According to corporate legend, as detailed on the company's website, the round top was the idea of a Weber Brothers employee, George Stephen, who was frustrated with the performance of the standard open-topped grill still found in public parks throughout America. To provide circulating heat, he cut up and reattached rounded parts of a buoy that his company manufactured for the u.s. Coast Guard and produced a new kind of grill.

An advertisement of 1952 for a rival product produced by Cook 'n' Tools referred back to the history of barbecue: 'Today's newest charcoal broiler combines all the qualities of the deep-pit barbecue; beehive oven of the Southwest Indians and the pioneer Dutch oven.'[20] Even Trader Vic, the American

Oil drum barbecue, Kansas City, mid-2000s.

apostle of Polynesian hedonism, allowed that a luau could take place around a kettle barbecue. For Vic, the most important equipment needed to recreate the luau was a glass of tropical punch and a laid-back smile.[21]

Other barbecue-hungry folks did not need to purchase Stephens's well-known kettle grill, preferring themselves to adapt oil drums to the noble purpose of grilling. A newspaper article of 1951 about the Burkes, a family from Corpus Christi, Texas, noted that they 'like to entertain with Ray's portable barbecue pit made out of an oil drum'. That Ray Burke, the father of the family, was a geologist for Union California Oil might explain his choice of materials.[22] Nobel Prize-winning author John Steinbeck was another who preferred the oil drum grill. Interviewed in the small backyard of his New York City home in 1953, Steinbeck 'strolled to the grill, an oil drum cut lengthwise and opened by a pulley so that it looked like an enormous pair of jaws'. Steinbeck's interviewer noted, 'I'd never seen an oil drum converted into a grill before.' On

Chicken, pork, and bacon-wrapped corn cook on different levels in a wood-fired smoker.

Pork ribs in a an industrial-scale smoker.

Steinbeck's grill, over a bed of charcoal, were 'three big lengths of spareribs and six huge potatoes wrapped in aluminum foil'.[23] In the West Indies, where oil barrels are also salvaged to make steel drums, oil drum barbecues are preferred for grilling many foods, including Jamaican jerk chicken.

In Cuba there is a form of barbecue known as the *caja china* or 'Chinese box', which incorporates something of each of oven, pit and rack barbecuing. (No one knows why it is called 'Chinese'. When interviewed by the *New York Times*, anthropologist Sidney Mintz surmised that the name might have had something to do with the 150,000 Chinese labourers who immigrated to Cuba in the middle of the nineteenth century.[24]) The *caja china* is a large metal box into which cooks place meat, usually a butterflied pig, that has been enclosed in a flat cage. Fuel, generally charcoal, is placed in the lid, which is recessed slightly into the top of the box. Keeping the heat source surrounding the pig speeds up the cooking time, so that roasting that would generally take ten hours can

A 'Little Chief' smoker for use in backyards.

be accomplished in as little as three. This method, however, keeps smoke and meat separate throughout the process, so it might be argued that this is not really barbecue, despite the fact that one fan called its results 'pig candy'.[25]

As barbecue technology has developed, with the goal of making the process easier and easier for backyard practitioners, a fierce debate has erupted over the use of gas grills. These work by providing a regulatable flame over which meat can

A pig on a spit at the annual Säubrennerkirmes pig roasting festival in Wittlich, Germany, *c.* 2008.

be roasted on a metal rack. Many feel that since gas fire does not produce smoke, this does not even qualify as barbecue. Others feel that the use of commercial charcoal provides an unpleasant and inauthentic flavour and that only wood creates the proper taste of smoke. In handling these debates and exploring barbecue – whether in poles, holes, racks or ovens – we hearken back to our opening definition of barbecue: slow smoke roasting.

4
A World of Barbecue

Wherever there is flesh and fire, there can be barbecue. Barbecue, slow smoke roasting, is a flexible technique. Regional variations of barbecue throughout the world integrate this shared cooking technique with locally available products, flavour palates and wood. A Jamaican goat rubbed with a paste of allspice, thyme, chilli, salt, ginger and lime juice and barbecued over pimento (allspice) and other woods yields jerk goat. Another goat just to the west on the world map, rubbed with oregano, lime juice and salt and cooked in a pit over mesquite, along with other wood, can make Mexican-style *cabrito*. Both, when properly executed, produce transcendent culinary experiences.

This list of combining local products and flavours before they hit the barbecue goes on: barbecued brisket (u.s.), planked salmon (u.s.), *lechon* (Philippines), *barbacoa de cabeza* (Mexico)*, kalua* pig (Polynesia), *sosaties* (South Africa), *char siu* (China), and many more, some cooked with variations on equipment and technology, but all cooked by barbecue, slow smoke roasting.

The essential barbecue cooking technique can be divided into three steps. The first is pre-seasoning, in which meat, fish or poultry is seasoned with a spice rub, paste, marinade or brine. Second, some hours after pre-seasoning, the item is slowly smoke roasted (barbecued) until tender. Doneness is determined by fork-tenderness. The meat should remain moist and yield to being pulled apart with a table fork. Third, during or after cooking, the meat is basted, mopped, dipped or glazed with some sauce to add moisture and flavour. These sauces often combine sweet and sour elements and spices.

Of these three steps, only the second is essential for barbecue.

Once a cook understands these three steps, the infinite possibilities of barbecue are apparent. Step one can incorporate any flavourings, step two any main item cooked over any wood, and step three any sauce. A barbecue cook, then, can distance herself from dogmatic recipes indicating precise amounts, temperatures, woods and smoking times and instead cook nearly everything in the same fashion: using available ingredients and her senses and instincts to determine flavour and doneness.

Food writer Elisabeth Rozin's concept of flavour profiles serves especially well to illustrate both the common core of barbecue and its infinite variations. Rozin identifies flavour principles as common elements to cuisine in various regions that give the foods of those regions distinct flavours. Soy sauce, chilli paste, sesame seeds and garlic, for example, may make something Korean-style; garlic, anchovy, tomato and olive oil give you a Sicilian flavour. By employing some of these combinations, cooks may be able to reference a region and vary dishes in ways that reflect a cultural logic. Rozin writes that 'Custom tradition and familiarity all invest certain flavoring combinations with meaning and with a positive value.'[1]

The following sampling from the world of barbecue (roughly two per continent) is not meant to be a comprehensive listing of all barbecue dishes – which is impossible in this small volume and complicated due to seemingly infinite regional and individual variations – but rather an illustration of the common core and rich diversity of barbecue preparations. While some recipes are provided in this book, using the three steps mentioned above can free the reader from following the recipe precisely: just pre-season the meat and barbecue with the wood of choice until fork-tender, basting periodically throughout cooking, or glaze with sauce at the end.

Africa

In southern Africa – South Africa as well as the neighbouring countries of Namibia, Zimbabwe, Zambia, Botswana and beyond – the term 'braai' is used instead of 'barbecue'. The full term is the Afrikaans *braaivleis*, roasted or barbecued meat, but in conversation 'braai' suffices. The Zulu term *shisa nyama* (burnt meat) is also used in a post-apartheid South Africa.

'Braai' doesn't refer to one specific kind of food preparation but is rather a term as all-encompassing as 'barbecue'. Braai challenges our definition of barbecue in that it can properly mean both direct grilling, commonly *boerewors* or other sausages, fish, chicken, steaks and kebabs, and true barbecue (slow smoke roasting), more likely of tougher cuts of meat such as ribs or *sosaties*, kebabs of mutton interspersed with onions, apricots and other ingredients.

Braai fires are typically made of charcoal or wood, providing good smoke flavour. Many woods are used, including fig, grape vines and varieties of acacia. As is true of barbecue throughout the world, hard woods are best.

Braai, like barbecue elsewhere, is often considered the domain of men. The stereotypical South African man stands

Barbecue on the waterfront in Stone Town, Zanzibar.

outside around the braai with other men drinking beer while their female companions handle the side dishes: salad, beverages and pap, a cornmeal porridge ubiquitous in Africa (though it goes by many other names as well). A spicy accompaniment can be found in *piri-piri* hot sauce or *chakalaka*, a spicy relish made from onions, tomatoes, chillies, peppers, spices and often canned baked beans for body. Braais are often potluck parties ('bring and braai') where friends bring various meats to be grilled and the host provides beverages (especially beer) and some side dishes.

Coupé-coupé is a catchall term for Central African barbecue, usually beef, but sometimes chicken or game. It is eaten across a band of Central Africa: Cameroon, Gabon, the Republic of Congo and the Democratic Republic of the Congo. Coupé-coupé as it is known today probably originated in the Republic of Congo (formerly French Congo) and, like many barbecue preparations, represents a fusion of indigenous ingredients and techniques with colonial influences. The term itself illustrates this fusion – it comes from the French *couper*, to cut, but is repeated, like many terms in Central Africa (*fufu*, porridge, and *kuku*, chicken, are two other food terms in that linguistic style). The name refers to the chopped or pulled state of the meat after barbecuing. Coupé-coupé is typically sold in outdoor markets or on the street in small packets of foil, along with a section of baguette with which to make a sandwich. In markets one typically sees beef or chicken, while game is common in home cooking or family gatherings.

Also illustrative of the merger of African technique with colonial influence is the key flavouring ingredient in coupé-coupé: Maggi-brand sauce, a now ubiquitous Nestlé product which dates back to the late nineteenth century. Following our familiar three steps, the meat is pre-seasoned with Maggi and other spices, usually chilli powder, barbecued while being basted with the juice from the marinade, and served with bread and hot sauce.[2]

East Asia

China has an abundance of barbecued meats (*siu mei* in Cantonese) – duck (*siu ngaap*), goose (*siu ngo*), pork shoulder (*siu yuk*), pork ribs and sausages – that are similarly often roasted in a gas or electric oven, but properly and historically would have been slowly smoke roasted: barbecued. Perhaps the greatest and saddest evidence of the widespread decline of Chinese barbecue in favour of cleaner and less flavour-imparting cooking equipment is the key ingredient in many Chinese barbecue recipes of today (especially for pork): red food colouring. Proper barbecue produces a red tint around the meat called

Sturgeon cooked on skewers on a small wood-burning grill in Turkmenestan.

Chinese barbecued duck, San Francisco.

a 'smoke ring'. In the absence of smoking, cooks add a garish colour with pigment.

Even today, though, real Chinese roasted meats are often barbecued. Cooks place smouldering charcoal in the bottom of a large metal roasting box (essentially a hybrid between an oven and a smokehouse) and roast the meat, which hangs from above, adding coals periodically. The predecessor to this charcoal and aluminum technology looked very similar – a wooden box heated with coals from wood. *Siu mei* originated in eastern China but is popular throughout the Chinese-speaking world. It is usually sold in restaurants for eating there or taking away.

Siu mei is the catch-all term for Chinese barbecued meats. *Char siu* (alternately spelled *cha siu*), perhaps the best known of the *siu mei*, is usually boneless pork, often from the collar (neck) or shoulder, marinated in hoisin sauce, soy sauce, five-spice powder, rice wine vinegar, honey and, yes, red food colouring, and barbecued. The same technique works for larger cuts such as ribs or large pieces of shoulder with a concomitant longer cooking time. Many people know *char siu* from its key role in the pork bun (*char siu bao*).

The Chinese take barbecue so seriously that the Beijing restaurant Kao Rou Ji, which has been in business since 1848, was recently awarded cultural heritage status on the basis of its barbecued lamb, a speciality of Muslim Chinese cuisine.

'Mongolian barbecue' is a restaurant mainstay of stir-fried bits of meat and vegetables. As mentioned before, though tasty, it is neither Mongolian, making its appearance on Taiwanese and Chinese restaurant menus in the 1970s and '80s, nor barbecue, given that it is cooked by sautéing or stir-frying on a griddle rather than by slow smoke roasting.

Aficionados often point to another Mongolian dish, *khorhog*, as *real* Mongolian barbecue. As previously discussed, to make *khorhog* an animal like goat or mutton is cut into pieces and placed in a pot with a bit of water and vegetables. Rocks are thoroughly heated on a fire and dropped in the pot, and the pot sealed, cooking the meat from inside the pot. Before eating, the rocks are removed. The attentive reader will no doubt notice that this cooking method is, more properly, steaming or stewing, and lacks two important elements to be considered true barbecue: smoke (beyond the smoke flavour carried by the rocks) and roasting.

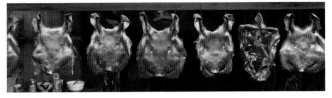

Smoked pig head, Hunan Province, China.

Although it is often referred to as Korean barbecue, *bulgogi* does not really qualify as barbecue because the meat is quickly grilled through contact with metal rather than smoke or radiant heat.

But there *is* Mongolian barbecue, *boodog*, cooked via a rather unique method, not unlike *khorhog*, but with the hide of the animal serving as the pot. Goat, lamb or, most famously, marmot is gutted (usually by removing the head of marmot or goat and taking out the guts through the head or rear) before the cavity is stuffed with hot rocks and, depending on the cook's preference, with some of the organs that were removed. Cooks (almost always men) then seal the cavity with wire while the animal cooks from the inside for a few hours until the rocks have cooled. Meanwhile the outside of the animal is singed and seared over a wood fire, removing the hair and crisping the skin, contributing smoke flavour. Increasingly a blowtorch substitutes for the fire, meaning that the animal is not truly barbecued, as neither the rocks nor the torch contribute smoke flavour. To serve, the animal is sliced open lengthwise. Inside the cavity is a soupy combination of fat, offal and liquid that is drunk first. The meat is eaten next, and if properly cooked can be pulled apart by hand.

A careful reader may have expected Korean barbecue (or Japanese *yakiniku*, for that matter) to be included in this section. After all, dishes like *bulgogi* and *kalbi* are served in restaurants worldwide and dubbed 'Korean barbecue'. Yet though it is delicious, it does not meet the definition of barbecue, as the meat is thinly sliced and quickly grilled without much smoke.

South and Central Asia

Tandoors are classically clay tube- or egg-shaped ovens used for cooking in India and throughout the subcontinent, Central Asia and parts of the Middle East. Its cousins include the tannur in the Arabic-speaking world and the tonir in Armenia. They are increasingly made from steel or other materials for

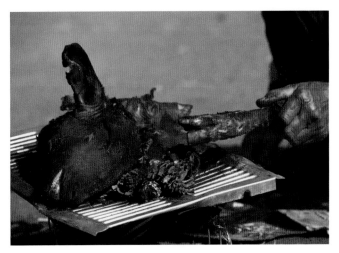

A barbecued goat head on the grill in Israel.

A chef for the Kandahar Restaurant at the luxury Oberoi Hotel, Mumbai, displays meat that has been cooked in a traditional tandoor oven.

Bedouin barbecue.

restaurant use, and may have electric or gas-burning heating elements. Many would not immediately think of tandoori cooking as barbecue – it is often done indoors in restaurants, the fire is not very visible, and 'tandoori' has become its own flavouring and cooking style referenced on menus, implying meats marinated in a yogurt-based spiced mixture and grilled on a skewer. But because this cooking can be done slowly over coals, it can be barbecue (though it is indeed often closer to grilling).

North America

In planking, a barbecue method from u.s. and Canada First Nations, the meat is placed on a soaked plank of wood (historically cypress in the u.s. Northwest and British Columbia, often misidentified as cedar and, more recently, real cedar), which slowly steams and smoulders as the fish cooks, adding additional flavour and supporting the tender flesh. The plank can then function as a plate for dining.

On the east coast of the U.S. planking is also used for cooking shad with a slightly different technique in times past: planks were preheated and the shad nailed to the planks and placed vertically around the fire, rotating them periodically. While both planked salmon and planked shad were served at large gatherings, planked shad dinners have become an annual political fundraising tradition in Virginia that continues today. In both cases, because salmon and shad are oily fish, the planks are reused and develop additional flavor over time from the fish oils.

The classic *barbacoa* of Mexico and Texas is done pit-style and perhaps best known for its barbecued cow head, *barbacoa de cabeza*, though it is also done with a whole sheep, goat or pig. It is popular in ranching regions of Mexico, especially in the north, and the Southwestern U.S., where there are large Mexican immigrant populations, but a type of *barbacoa* can be found throughout Mexico and Central America. To generalize, in the north, beef head (*cabeza*) or goat (*cabrito*) are common, with lamb popular in central Mexico and pork (*cochinita pibil*) in the Yucatan peninsula. At home it is often cooked by men who begin the process on Saturday night in a backyard. The meat is slow roasted overnight and eaten on Sunday as tacos with corn tortillas, salsa and toppings like chilli, lime, coriander and sliced onion.

To cook *barbacoa* one digs a hole in the ground and lights a wood fire in the hole. Mesquite is often used in desert regions, though the flavour is strong, so it is often blended with other hardwood. When the fire is mostly coals, the meat or head is seasoned with salt, pepper and sometimes chilli, wrapped in burlap, or with banana or agave leaves, depending on the region, often along with onions, garlic, lime halves or other flavouring ingredients and buried in the pit on top of the coals. It then cooks overnight. While not necessary for a successful outcome, some cooks include a pot of water (sometimes flavoured with onion, garlic and chilli) in the pit to steam the meat and catch the juices. This liquid can then be eaten as a soup or used to cook beans with a profound flavour. *Barbacoa* is sold in restaurants or served for festive occasions but is also popular among backyard barbecuers.

Like many things American, U.S. barbecue is a mixture of Old and New World traditions and ingredients. The Southern novelist Pat Conroy has declared that 'there are no ideas in the South, just barbecue.' The meats, most often pork and beef, are from the Old World; the barbecue cooking method and some predominant seasonings, like chilli and tomato-based sauces, are from the New. Sometimes the work has revolutionary potential, as a character in Conroy's novel *The Prince of Tides* claims of his own mother's cooking: 'She did magic things with pork and changed the way I looked at the flesh of pigs forever. If she had published her recipe for pit barbecue, it would have altered the quality of life in the South as we knew it.'[3]

While barbecue can be found throughout the States, the 'barbecue belt' runs from the Southern U.S. – the Carolinas, Georgia, Tennessee and Kentucky – to the Southwest and southern Midwest – Texas, Oklahoma and Missouri. Roughly speaking, pork is favoured in the East and beef in the West, with a small pocket of mutton barbecue preferred in Kentucky. Scholars and aficionados have worked to classify distinct and sometimes contradictory barbecue regions based on the preferred cuts of meat and predominant sauce characteristics. While there are countless exceptions and variations to confound this table, in broad outline:

Table 3: Traditional Meat and Sauce Combinations in u.s. Barbecue

Region	Meat	Sauce
Eastern North Carolina	Whole hog	Vinegar-based
Western North Carolina	Pork shoulder	Tomato-based
South Carolina	Pork	Mustard-based
Kansas City	Beef and pork (but especially pork ribs)	Tomato- and molasses-based
Memphis	Beef and pork (but especially pork ribs)	Dry spice rub or tomato-based
Owensboro, Kentucky	Mutton	Vinegar-based

Barbecue in the u.s. has a long tradition in festivals and especially political fundraisers in the South. Politicians would demonstrate their largesse by hosting 'pig pickins', where voters would fill their plates by picking shreds of meat from a whole barbecued hog. Today the tradition continues at parties and gatherings such as family reunions. While some u.s. cooks produce barbecue at home, most is cooked for large parties or at informal restaurants where barbecue can be eaten there or taken home.

Another particularly American feature of barbecue is that it is not just a delicious food or entrepreneurial venture. The u.s. also boasts sanctioned competitions with elaborate rulebooks and scoring criteria, making barbecue a sport as well as a dish.

Central and South America

The somewhat unusual English term 'jerk' probably has the same origin as 'jerky', the Spanish *charqui*, a salted dried meat popular throughout South America. While jerk might have been closer to *charqui* in the past, saltier and drier than its current version, jerk today is barbecued from fresh meat. Often this is goat or chicken legs, but beef, pork and fish are also jerked.

Like 'barbecue', 'jerk' is a multifaceted term that can be used to describe the seasoning, the cooking method and the finished dish. Jerk can be found in many parts of the Caribbean but has become a national dish of Jamaica and is often referred to as 'Jamaican jerk'. While there are infinite variations, there are a few key elements to any jerk seasoning: a marinade paste comprised of allspice (pimento), Scotch bonnet (habenero) chillies, thyme, spring onions, lime juice, ginger and any number of other ingredients, and barbecuing over a fire that includes allspice wood.

Historically pits or open fires were used for jerking but in recent times an icon of jerk is the oil drum barbecue grill, made from an oil drum split lengthwise and affixed to legs, with the other half of the drum used as a cover. Jerk can be made at home and packaged jerk pastes and sauces are available, but most jerk is purchased from roadside stands or restaurants.

The central feature of a South American *asado* is a large fire around which whole or half animals, usually cattle, are split open, affixed to stakes and barbecued, often over a period of many hours or even more than a day to allow the whole animal

Argentinian barbecue: sheep roasting near a fire in a typical *parrilla* restaurant in Patagonia.

to fully cook (called *asado al palo*). The meat is accompanied by bread, salad and *chimichurri* sauce, a vinegar-based sauce with many variations but usually including vegetable oil or olive oil, garlic, parsley and sometimes chilli.

Asado, like barbecue, can also be a more general term for the quicker grilling of sausages, steaks and other items over wood coals or even a gas grill. *Asado* is often associated with Argentina, though it is cooked throughout South America, including Uruguay, Paraguay, Chile and Brazil. Its Brazilian counterpart is called *churrasco*. A traditional *asado* is a mixed grill that includes chorizo, blood sausage, sweetbreads, ribs and steaks.

Asado differs from other barbecue in that traditionally the meat is not dry rubbed or marinated before cooking, but rather cooked plain (or lightly salted) with salt added after cooking.

Churrasco is a term for barbecue used in South America, which sometimes refers to the *asado* method and sometimes to roasting meats on a grill, often on skewers.

Men from the former Yugoslavia roasting pigs on spits.

Europe

Lechon is a barbecued suckling pig. The term derives from *leche*, milk, and implies that the pig is young enough to be suckling. While most cultures that breed pigs have some sort of roast baby pig tradition, Spain's colonization of much of the world helped make *lechon* a traditional dish far beyond the country's borders. It can be found throughout the Spanish-speaking world – Spain, the Caribbean, Central and South America and especially the Philippines, where it has become a signature dish, seasoned with salt, pepper, garlic and soy sauce.

To cook *lechon* traditionally the pig is gutted and impaled lengthwise on a metal spit and roasted rotisserie-style over a charcoal or wood fire. It is still cooked that way, especially for

Lechon for sale, Rio Piedras, Puerto Rico, 1942.

festivals and parties. Increasingly electric or gas-fire rotisserie ovens are used in commercial environments such as restaurants.

Throughout Eastern Europe whole animals, especially lamb, are spit roasted over wood or charcoal fires for festivals and special occasions. Suckling pig prepared in this manner is also popular. The art of spit roasting lies in crisping the skin without burning it and fully cooking the inside of the animal as it roasts.

Because of its religious connotation and seasonality, spit-roasted lamb is an especially popular Easter dish in Greece and throughout Christian Eastern Europe, including Croatia, Lithuania, Serbia and Bulgaria. Halal versions of the same dish are consumed at other times of year throughout Muslim Eastern Europe. While there are many regional variations, the meat is usually simply prepared with salt, pepper and sometimes oregano and/or lemon juice before roasting and

Barbecuing sardines in Lisbon during a street festival.

then cooked until crisp. The meat is eaten with bread and often also with raw crisp spring vegetables, such as radishes and spring onions (scallions).

On the Mediterranean island of Cyprus, a special combination of rotisserie and barbecue known as *souvla* has fed large crowds for many centuries. Elevated troughs are filled with coals and multiple large pieces of meat and/or whole birds are suspended over the heat on a spit, which is regularly rotated by hand. The meat is brushed with olive oil and spices while cooking but is otherwise unadorned, being served simply with salad and bread.

Oceania and the Pacific

In the Pacific Islands whole roast pig is a popular feast item. While there are many terms and variations throughout the Pacific Islands, Hawaiian-style *kalua* pig is probably the best known, largely due to the tourist industry and its prominent place at the luau.

As described previously, a *kalua* pig is pit roasted in an underground oven or *imu*. The pig is wrapped in banana and/ or ti leaves and chicken wire (so it doesn't fall apart) and sometimes stuffed with hot stones (not unlike the *boodog* method) before being buried under additional leaves, wet burlap and earth and left to steam among the rocks and coals. Shredded banana wood provides additional smoke over the long cooking process, usually overnight. *Kalua* pork (as opposed to *kalua* pig) is cooked in a similar fashion or is barbecued above ground but doesn't incorporate the whole pig – usually just a shoulder.

Kalua pig is classically served pulled at luaus and other feasts along side *poi* and *lomi-lomi* salmon (a salted salmon and tomato salad). Like other forms of barbecue, sadly, ersatz *kalua* pig

Luau cooks stuff a pig carcass with hot rocks and wrap it in leaves before lowering it into the pit to roast.

Barbecue sign, Corpus Christi, Texas, 1939.

recipes using pressure cookers with liquid smoke added or home ovens abound.

While Australia is often associated with barbecue, it is primarily a quick grilling tradition: sausages, steaks, chicken, vegetables, hamburgers and fish, along with the Australian specialities ostrich, emu, crocodile and kangaroo, accompanied by a large volume of beer. In the 1980s the Australian Tourism Commission aired an advertisement in which the actor Paul Hogan offered to 'slip an extra shrimp on the barbie' for visiting Americans, forever associating Australia with one grilled crustacean in the popular imagination.

However, in New Zealand Maori tradition there is true pit barbecue, called *hangi* (as in the expression 'putting down a *hangi*'), which is still practised today. Meat and vegetables are typically wrapped in leaves or muslin or placed in shallow pans and buried in the coals. Must-have foods include sweet potatoes and onions in addition to meat. A Maori legend tells of a fleet-footed hero, Te Houtaewa, whose mother sent him to fetch some kumaras, local sweet potatoes, for the *hangi*. She supposed he would go to the nearest garden, but instead he sped off in the direction of another far-off village where he stole kumaras from their storage pit, faced down the whole village and escaped home, all in the time that it took to heat up the *hangi*. There is now a series of foot races named for this sneaky character in northern New Zealand.

Whether acquired on the sly from neighbours or markets, the foods are layered in a wire or grid-like *hangi* basket, with longer-cooking food like meat placed at the bottom, closer to the heat. Like other forms of pit barbecue, in putting down a *hangi* long-burning hardwood is essential, along with volcanic stones. Sometimes steel and iron rods or lumps are included to retain the heat in the pit. *Hangi*, like other forms of barbecue, has begun to inspire competition, including a fusion *hangi* contest held in Auckland in 2011.

5
Competition and Connoisseurship

In much of the world barbecue is a menu item, a special occasion dish or a central item at a feast or family gathering. In North America, however, especially since the Second World War, barbecue has become a subculture unto itself, complete with music, legendary restaurants and international competitions throughout the u.s. and Canada. Barbecue plays a starring role in cable television shows on several networks and competition barbecue is showcased on the Learning Channel's popular show *BBQ Pitmasters*. Increasingly, perhaps due to this wide coverage, competitions can be found beyond North America as well.

Competition Barbecue

The origins of competition barbecue in the u.s. are as futilely sought and almost as frequently debated as the site of the 'first' barbecue. Like barbecue itself, barbecue competitions are a simple concept that probably evolved in multiple locations, at multiple times, whenever one person said to another, 'My barbecue is better than yours.'

Competitions in the u.s. today are huge public events, often accompanied by food for sale to the public, live music

Barbecue Guinness World Record Event, Asunción, Paraguay, 2008.

and games and amusements. The largest of these events, the Memphis in May World Championship Barbecue Contest, claims on its website to generate over $30 million for Memphis each year.

Barbecue competitions have existed for decades as formal offshoots of county, regional or state fairs, and informally for much longer as fundraisers and unofficial get-togethers.[1] It is only in the last 30-odd years, however, that the competition barbecue as a national phenomenon has really taken hold. While there are many individuals and organizations responsible for the growth of competition barbecue, the Memphis in May festival has generated a tremendous amount of press, first by hosting the championship competition since 1980, and then by sanctioning a network of regional competitions across the country. A number of organizations, such as the Kansas City Barbeque Society and the National Barbecue Association, are similarly structured, sanctioning regional competitions and uniting the regional winners at a national competition at season's end. Teams typically participate in the competitions of various different societies, which each have particular rules, meat categories, judging criteria and procedures. Regardless of the sanctioning body of each competition, the prize is money and a chance for advancement into additional competitions which are only open to invitees. Often the money is significant, topping u.s.$10,000 per event, and contestants may enter multiple events. This prize money is raised through competition fees, admission charges for the public and sponsorship, making competition not only a hobby but an investment.

Multi-lamb roast in China.

Masculinity

While women do compete in barbecue, one of the pervasive themes of competition barbecue culture is masculinity. Barbecue elegantly embraces several stereotypically Guy Things: fire building, beast slaughtering, fiddling with grubby mechanical objects, expensive gear fetishes, afternoon-long beer drinking, and, of course, great heaps of greasy meat at the end of the day. Top this off with the frisson of ritual tribal warfare and you've got the mother of all male pastimes.[2]

One competition barbecue cook explained:

> It's the caveman in us. I think that's why you see more and more men barbecuing. It's a macho thing. Playing with fire and being outdoors, bragging about how good you cook, it's got all the macho rush to it without any of the violence.[3]

Terms like 'caveman', 'Neanderthal' and 'macho' abound in explanations of the relationship between men and barbecue. The prehistoric simplicity of barbecue should not be ignored. Barbecuing requires no utensils and little mediation from human or material. The essential ingredients are fire, meat and an appropriate proximity between the two. Everything else – seasoning, off-set cast-iron smoker, digital thermometer, sauce or even tending the meat as it cooks – is simply garnish.

Men across cultures savour not only the flavour of barbecue but its process – standing in the outdoors, chatting with friends, drinking beer or something stronger, building and tending a fire, hauling, cutting, rubbing and hoisting whole animals or large cuts of meat and, perhaps most importantly,

Gran Asado event celebrating 200 years of Argentine self-government at Esher Rugby and Football Club, Hersham, Britain, 2010.

waiting and anticipating the succulent results at the intersection of fire and flesh. Barbecue done right is a day-long process or more. Like baking, it isn't something that can be tweaked countless times during the process – it is started and let go. It is also cooked relatively infrequently by amateur cooks – perhaps at most once every few weeks in season. Accordingly, it is special occasion food that takes a long time to learn and a lifetime to master. Secrets are carefully guarded and shared with team members, close friends or family.

Some of this mystery is key to the phenomenon of competition barbecue. Within relatively strict guidelines detailing the allowable meat, presentation, saucing and fuel, how do you cook a simple thing exceptionally well and in a way that distinguishes itself from the competition?

The Performance of Barbecue: Athleticism

Competition barbecue is hardly a sport in the conventional sense. There is a lot of sitting around, drinking beer and sports drinks, talking and listening to music, and very occasional strenuous physical activity, such as icing drinks with 50-lb bags of ice, carrying six 10-lb pork shoulders from the meat truck or stooping at an odd angle to get the fire going. It may seem even more ridiculous to think that a competition devoted to sedentary activity and the consumption of fatty meats, where competition seeds become available due to coronaries rather than injury, is anything but loafing. But in many ways sport and athleticism are important aspects of the performance of competition barbecue, which involves two full days of sun, smoke, heat and physical activity as well as, for smaller teams without distinct shifts, hourly waking throughout the night to check the meat and fire. It can be exhausting to the uninitiated.

Even casual observation at the competitions reveals many markers of sport. Many teams have team uniforms, even have two sets of uniforms: a practice T-shirt, which they wear for cooking during the weekend, and a 'game time' golf shirt for judging and awards ceremonies. Many teams have 'Pit Crew' emblazoned across their shirts, identifying them as a barbecue pit team member in a direct analogy to another sport with pits, auto racing. These teams are often the more entrepreneurial ones that sell T-shirts without the 'Pit Crew' designation to fans and visitors.

Like an organized sport, these competitions are held in conspicuous spectator-oriented places. The logical place to hold a competition for outdoor cookery might be a field or car park adjacent to a building, which could potentially provide water, electricity, toilets and shelter for the cooks. What we see instead are competitions held as major tourist attractions, downtown rejuvenation activities, chamber of commerce-sponsored events in small towns or fundraisers for fire stations and other non-profit organizations. Though the competition cooks do not typically offer tastes of their food, and indeed at some competitions are forbidden by local public health departments from doing so, these competitions are spectator events. Unfortunately, for the most part there is not much to see. Of the 36 or more hours of a competition, actual food handling might only take two or three hours. For the remaining time meats cook slowly in a closed cooker. As a consequence, the actual 'event' for the spectators often consists of commercially vended barbecue and other foods, live music, a beer garden at some competitions, seeing the awards ceremony and glimpsing the teams in action. The teams, unable to show much 'action', sometimes sell sauces, rubs or memorabilia if allowed, and decorate their site to differentiate themselves from their competition.

The spectators' role at the competitions does much to change the dynamic of the team from one of pure recreation and competitive spirit to one of crowd-pleaser. Many teams use creative team names, visual puns especially using hogs, pigs, swine or similar words, signage, trophies, elaborate rigs and memorabilia to draw interest in their site. Others, especially small teams with less time to spare, tend to discourage tourist traffic by maintaining a relatively low profile through a more utilitarian design and minimal signage.

While spectators are usually not allowed to sample competitive meats, judges are required to, a fact that makes this an increasingly popular hobby. As a *New York Times* article reported in 2007, an increase in the number of competitions means that more judges are needed, which in turn leads to opportunities for seasoned judges to train others in the arts of critical connoisseurship. Aspirants to judgeship must study a competition rule book, swear to a code of conduct and taste a lot of barbecue. Once certified as competent to judge, 'Barbecue judges are not paid, but many believe that the smoked meat they consume – about two pounds at each contest – is fair compensation.'[4]

Sociologist and essayist John Shelton Reed recalled his experience as a judge of the World Championship Barbecue Cooking Contest. As it was his first time judging, he listened eagerly as

> Our instructor began with the basics ('If you don't eat pork, please let us know') and moved on to matters of comportment ('Stay sober until *after* the judging') and ethics ('If your ex-wife's boyfriend is on a team, you should disqualify yourself').[5]

While Reed judged meats at the world's most famous competition in Memphis, there are thousands of others in the United States as well as in other countries. The Irish city of Limerick, for example, has hosted an international barbecue competition as part of its annual Riverfest, with teams from over 50 countries. Richmond, British Columbia, hosts an annual Canadian Festival of Chili and BBQ. A barbecue and *lechon asado* competition was held in San Juan, Puerto Rico, in 2010, and in 2006 an *asado* contest in Buenos Aires drew 5,000 spectators. Braai competitions are common in southern Africa and even in Britain, where they cheer up homesick expats.

Barbecue made its way into a different kind of competition in 2007 when the French team competing for the Bocuse d'or, an international cooking contest named for haute cuisine hero Paul Bocuse, took third place with a menu that included barbecued foie gras.

Showmanship

Night Help? Rover's Hind Leg East? Pan Handle Smokers? Smokin Jokin? Aunt Jean's Barbecue? Barbecue Country? Fuhgeddaboutit? Mad Max? Fire Starters? Smoke Encounters of the Third Swine? Ribs by Andy? Smitty's Bar B Q? J DC's Soon-to-be Famous Shotgun House Rib Rub? Roland Porkers?

This roll call at a barbecue competition introduces a dichotomy that runs as an undercurrent throughout the competition barbecue world. There is levity, a considerable amount of self-parody and a high social value placed on the 'sport' of competition barbecue, as reflected by the team names, while at the same time these teams are investing huge sums of time, money and energy into the competition and want to win prize money, esteem and entry into national forums. At the conclusion of a cook's meeting late in the season, a contest organizer summarizes this dichotomy in his conclusion to the meeting, 'All you new teams, if you have any questions, there's a lot of teams here that have done this competition before. Ask 'em. There's not a team here that won't help you out. I strongly recommend, however that you *not* accept any unsolicited cooking advice.' One competitor yells from the back of the tent, 'Hey, I hear the judges like things really black and charred this year.'

The other tension is that teams have to take competition very seriously to succeed but also have to be public educators and crowd-pleasers. Teams can be in a difficult situation in that they need the public for the cash prizes garnered from admission fees, public support for permits and street closings to accommodate the competitions, and visibility, especially valuable to the corporate sponsors, but they are really there to compete rather than to entertain.

Design and Gadgetry

All competition barbecue teams need to be organized. They are sometimes competing hundreds of miles from their homes, have a ten-minute window of time in which to submit their entries for foods that take hours or even days to prepare and often operate in locations without access to supplies. Indeed, that is one reason why teams, despite being competitors, support each other so much. Everyone forgets *something* sometimes – paper towels, plastic bags, garbage bags, brushes, knives and dishes move graciously from rig to rig. Some teams use checklists, Post-it notes and timers to keep themselves on schedule, but others take organization to a new level.

In the week before a competition one team's organizer distributes a large spreadsheet file to the team by email. The heart of the file is a Gantt chart with a bar for each member of the team and a timeline from competition commencement to finish. Each team member is assigned a shift and at various times throughout each shift are tasks: '3:00 Start Cooker, 5:00 Start Shoulders, 8:00 Rotate Shoulders, 5:00 Foil Shoulders', and so on. From this chart team members know days in advance who they will be working with, what they will be expected to do and who will be working the other shifts. Another page of the file itemizes each piece of equipment every team member is expected to bring, and still another shows the schematic floor plan of the site setup, drawn to scale using architectural tools. A master copy of these spreadsheets is kept in a fat binder that contains recipes, instructions, photographs, logistical information such as directions, parking permits and hotel reservation numbers, and nearly every other bit of information imaginable – not that that precludes mistakes in competition.

In much the same way that the team emphasizes organization and thought, so does gadgetry play an important role in the mythology of the competition barbecue team, at times with a similar deference to the equipment in favour of the sensory considerations of the food itself. A neighbouring team has a police light on a timer so that every 45 minutes, no matter where on the grounds they are, someone is reminded to baste the meat. One team's new addition in gadgetry is a set of digital thermometers that wirelessly transmit temperature data to a remote location, further enhanced by high- and low-range alarms for when the cooker or meat reach a certain temperature. Says one competitor, 'With this baby I can be asleep in the hotel room and be woken up when the meat's done.'

Given that barbecuing is supposed to be a leisure activity, the amount of complicated technology used to reduce the amount of work necessary does seem to verge on the ridiculous. The team spends hours standing, sitting, talking, drinking and checking thermometers. Were the last part not necessary, they could *really* be doing the rest anywhere. That is to say, if every logical convenience were incorporated, the team would do what one competitor jokingly suggested (a *reductio ad absurdum*) – buy barbecue and submit it for judging, saving them time, money and energy. Far beyond its origins as a practical way to preserve fresh meat, barbecue has evolved into a unique experience woven of ritual, skill and humour, long-smoked and tender.

6
Sauces and Sides

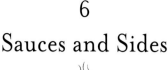

The authors of this book share the credo of chef Jason Sheehan, whose contribution to a collection titled *This I Believe* was 'I believe – *I know* – there is no such thing as too much barbecue.' But just because one can't get enough barbecue does not necessarily mean that barbecue is enough on its own. Although the term strictly applied refers only to a particular process of meat preparation, for many across the world, barbecue also suggests certain accessories in the form of sauces and sides that complete the experience. As Sheehan averred, 'good barbecue needs sides the way good blues need rhythm.' These sides vary significantly across cultures and regions, as does the use and composition of sauces. Thus we bring this exploration of barbecue to an end by expanding the focus a little further out to the edges of the plate.

Sauces

Within the North American barbecue tradition there are three separate and ferociously defended notions of the proper base for sauce: tomato, vinegar and mustard. The most widely recognized style, found bottled in all supermarkets, is the Kansas City style, which is tomato-based, thick and sweet, with a vinegar kick and varying degrees of spice and chilli-generated heat. In Kansas City's most famous establishments the sauce is served on the side, usually in squeeze bottles on the table so as not to distract attention from the glory of the smoked meat.

Texans also employ a tomato-based sauce, but it is thinner and tends to be much more vinegary than the Kansas City standard. It is known as 'mop sauce' since it is 'mopped' onto meat during cooking. It may also be served on finished meats in small quantities. The closer the grill is to Mexico, the more likely the mop sauce is to include spicing traditionally associated with that region, including cumin and chilli. One writer for the Depression-era Federal Writers' Project claimed,

> This sauce is as much part of the Latin heritage of the Southwest as are the crumbling Spanish Missions. Along the Rio Grande it is a dark crimson blend of tomatoes and chili peppers with the latter so hot and strong that a drop of it spilled on the table, will leave a charred spot after it is wiped away.[1]

Vinegar-based sauce predominates in North Carolina and is used to baste meats while they smoke, rather than as a condiment when they are ready to serve. Mustard-based sauce is the speciality of central and eastern South Carolina, where it imbues the 'cue with an arresting yellow hue that some outsiders find too strange to approach. Sometimes prepared with beer, this sauce has its origins in the German communities who settled in South Carolina in the eighteenth century. In both North and South Carolina meat is often served on buns shredded, or 'pulled', rather than in chunks, as is the more usual custom in Kansas City and through much of Texas.

While most of the nation (mustard-based fans aside) consumes barbecue in sauces with more or less tomato and more or less vinegar, a notable exception is the mayonnaise-based sauce sporting vinegar and lemon juice, but no tomato, used in Alabama as a basting and dipping sauce. Although this variation shocks many Americans, it is not really so different from one of the world's oldest barbecue sauces, the yoghurt marinade with which meat is usually treated before being cooked in a tandoor oven. That sauce, made with yoghurt, spices and, frequently, lemon juice, also imparts both moistness and a tart flavour to smoked meat, and has gained the approval of millions of diners over thousands of years.

East Asian barbecue traditions are in some ways similar to the Texan 'mop sauce' style. Chinese *char siu* is treated with a marinade before cooking that is typically based in hoisin sauce, thinned with sherry and vinegar. Hoisin has a black-bean paste base mixed with honey or brown sugar and vinegar and spiced to taste. Meat is typically served without the sauce, but when it is shredded and enclosed in a bun (not unlike a Carolinian pulled pork sandwich) it receives an extra coating of sauce. In Japanese tradition, too, sauce is used for basting. Typically teriyaki sauce, a sweetened soy-based sauce mixed with rice wine, is brushed lightly on chicken or beef before it is grilled to impart a subtle flavour of salt and sweet to smoked meats, which are then served plain or with a thickened version of teriyaki sauce.

While South American *asado* is typically prepared without any marinade aside from a salt rub and no mopping, it is often served with a brilliant green sauce called *chimichurri*, which is composed of chopped herbs (parsley, basil and coriander (cilantro) among the possibilities) mixed with vinegar, garlic and chilli. The sauce is dolloped on when the meat is served, counteracting the smoke of the meat with a fresh tang of greens and bite of hot chilli pepper.

A close relative of *chimichurri* is *piri piri* sauce, used across the Atlantic Ocean in Africa. The two sauces both originate in Iberian colonization of the Americas and Africa. *Piri piri* sauce also mixes chopped herbs with garlic, chillies and oil, using lemon juice instead of vinegar to provide piquancy and fore-grounding peppers rather than herbs, as chimichurri does. *Piri piri* sauce is typically orange while chimichurri is green. The bird's eye peppers that are the dominant flavouring of *piri piri* were first brought to Africa by Portuguese traders who had first encountered them through the colonization of South America, where the peppers are a native plant.

While *piri piri* sauce is primarily found in Angola and Mozambique, regions that were formerly colonized by Portugal, barbecue in the Congo and neighbouring Central African regions is noted for its use of Maggi sauce, as previously mentioned. Invented in Switzerland in the later nineteenth century, and used as a soup base in Europe, Maggi is used as a marinade in Congolese barbecue, adding an umami-rich layer of flavour to the smoked meats known as coupé-coupé.

Sides

Although meat has typically been highly valued as a menu item, there are nonetheless many dishes associated with barbecue that have no meat in them at all. In some cases these are very simple, as in the case of the crusty French bread served with coupé-coupé, but in others they are a little more elaborate.

In the Texas barbecue tradition there is 'the holy trinity of barbecue sides: beans, coleslaw and potato salad'.[2] The beans are baked kidney (pinto) beans, which differ from traditional New England baked beans in that cooks often use barbecue sauce as well as tough ends of barbecued meat to flavour them, either using commercially produced sauce or making their own. Coleslaw and potato salad are both creations of perpetual variation but tend to have mayonnaise-based creamy dressings. Sides are usually savoury, although one author's South Carolinian spouse was quick to identify banana pudding as an essential side to his state's barbecue.

Cornbread of greater and lesser sweetness is also widely considered an appropriate accompaniment to Southern barbecue, but will not be found in Kansas City, where soft white bread predominates on barbecue plates. In the Carolinas, kaiser rolls are the favoured vehicle for shredded barbecue meat.

One barbecue chronicler reported that it was traditional in Kansas in the 1930s to cook a stew made up of the parts of

South African barbecued bread (*roosterkoek*).

the steer that were not being barbecued – hearts, livers, kidneys and intestines – mixed with chopped potatoes, tomatoes and chillies. The dish, which was thickened with cornmeal in the final stage of cooking, was known in some parts as 'Son of a Bitch Stew' and in others as 'Prosecuting Attorney'.[3]

Much like American barbecuers, South African braai enthusiasts also consider beans-in-sauce and potato salad perfect accompaniments to smoked meat. *Sousboontjies*, a popular side dish for braai, is a dish made from a variety of white bean called sugar beans cooked with sugar and vinegar and served either hot or cold as a salad.

South African potato salad includes chopped onions and mayonnaise. Some South Africans prefer a potato 'bake' with their braai, baking slices of potatoes covered in a creamy sauce to serve alongside their meat. Another notable speciality of braai cooking is *roosterkoek*, stiff bread dough cooked on the grill to produce smoked rolls. A braai may also feature cooking in a large three-legged cast-iron pot called a *potjie*, which has its roots in the history of the Afrikaaner settlers. *Potjiekos* are the stews created in these cauldrons, which sit on top of smouldering coals to slow cook their ingredients, typically a mixture of vegetables.

Caribbean *lechoneras*, which sell large pieces of barbecued pig, also offer a wide range of side dishes. Customers typically find several different preparations of rice – boiled or fried – and an assortment of root vegetables, pickles and, especially at Christmas time, *pasteles*, small savoury turnovers perfected in Puerto Rican kitchens. Variations on the Puerto Rican *mofongo*, a dish of mashed plantains stuffed with seafood, vegetables or meat and piled up on the plate, are also found in most *lechoneras*. South American *asado*, on the other hand, is usually enjoyed unaccompanied, except by simple fresh salads dressed in vinaigrette and, in Argentina and Chile, some local red wine.

Meats cooked in tandoors in the South Asian barbecue tradition are usually served with stews or curries typically made with spice pastes and vegetables. They are accompanied at the table with a variety of breads, some also cooked in the tandoor, that can be used to hold grilled meats and sop up sauces and piquant chutneys. In cultures like those of South Asia, where barbecue is a common method of cooking rather than for special events or a cuisine mostly encountered in commercial enterprises, side dishes have no set identities. Chinese barbecued pork, for example, is typically a store-bought delicacy, since few homes have the space and equipment for the required smoking boxes. Eaten at home or at a restaurant table, it may be accompanied by a wide variety of dishes according to personal taste.

In cultures where sides are plentiful, they may serve a special function, allowing vegetarians the opportunity to participate in the camaraderie that seems to be the secret ingredient that defines and unites global barbecue. As the American writer Zora Neale Hurston once wished, 'Maybe all of us who do not have the good fortune to meet or meet again, in this world, will meet at a barbecue.'[4]

Recipes

Historical Recipes

Although barbecue has primarily been part of the folk foodways that are seldom recorded in print, some recipes did make their way into formal cookbooks in the nineteenth century, including a few, like Edwin Troxell Freedley's, that obviously diverge from the rules by using a regular oven rather than a pit, spit or grill. While the hole-in-the-ground tradition received ample respect through the twentieth century, occasional lapses occurred, as in Crisco's 'Noodle Barbecue' and attention sometimes strayed, especially under Trader Vic's guidance, from the food to the drink.

Barbecued Sheep

—Mrs Ella Turner, in *Buckeye Cookery*, ed. Estelle Woods Wilcox
(Minneapolis, MN, 1877)

Dig a hole in ground, in it build a wood fire, and drive four stakes or posts just far enough away so they will not burn; on these build a rack of poles to support the carcass. These should be of a kind of wood that will not flavor the meat. When the wood in the pit has burned to coals, lay sheep on rack, have a bent stick with a large sponge tied on one end, and the other fastened on one corner of the rack, and turn so that it will hang over the mutton; make a mixture of ground mustard and vinegar, salt and pepper, add sufficient water to fill the sponge the necessary number of times, and let it drip over the meat until done; have another fire burning near from which to add coals as they are needed.

Barbecued Rabbit or Squirrel
—Edwin Troxell Freedley, *Home Comforts: or, Things Worth Knowing in Every Household* (Philadelphia, PA, 1879)

Clean and wash the rabbit, which must be plump and young, and having opened it all the way on the under side, lay it flat, with a small plate or saucer to keep it down, in salted water for half an hour. Wipe dry and broil whole, with the exception of the head, when you have gashed across the backbone in eight or ten places, that the heat may penetrate this, the thickest part. Your fire should be hot and clear, the rabbit turned often. When browned and tender, lay upon a very hot dish, pepper and salt and butter profusely, turning the rabbit over and over to soak up the melted butter. Cover and set in the oven for five minutes, and heat in a tin cup two tablespoonfuls of vinegar, seasoned with one of made mustard. Anoint the hot rabbit well with this, cover, and send to table garnished with crisped parsley.

The odor of this barbecue is most appetizing, and the taste not a whit inferior. Squirrels may be barbecued in the same manner.

The American Barbecue
—Jessup Whitehead, *The Steward's Handbook and Guide to Party Catering* (Chicago, IL, 1889)

It is commonly called roasting oxen or other animals whole; the word itself is French barb-a-que, 'from head to tail,' [sic] but in practice so many disappointments occur through the meat coming from the bars burnt to a coal on the outside and too raw to be eaten inside, that those who have had experience take care to roast only quarters or sides. The way it is done is the same in the beginning as the clam bake; a trench is dug in the ground and a wood fire made in it. When it has burned about six hours and the pit bottom is covered with a bed of glowing coals and red hot rocks, instead of the covering up in sea weed as at the clam bake, some bars of iron are laid across the pit, making a monster grid-iron. Perhaps the iron can be obtained from the village blacksmith, or some old rails from the railroad, or two or three rails and small iron for cross-bars. Whole sheep and lambs can be roasted very well over such a bed of coals, also small pigs, chickens, 'possums, turkeys and such small animals, but oxen are better cut in quarters, as in that case it does not take more than an hour or two to cook them sufficiently. Occasions requiring a resort to the barbecue are constantly arising, either political or otherwise, for anniversaries, camp meetings, celebrations of various descriptions, and it only needs the trench to be dug the longer to give cooking facilities in the meat line to an indefinite extent; the bread is easily baked at a distance and hauled to the spot. But the great trouble experienced generally is to get the provisions divided among the people after the cooking; if this is not well managed two or three persons will drag a quarter of beef from the fire into the dust of the ground, hack off their few slices and leave the rest in such a condition that it is almost if not quite lost.

Birthday Barbecue

—Dorothy Dix, in *Dishes and Beverages of the Old South*,
ed. Martha McCulloch Williams (New York, 1913)

As refined gold can be gilded, barbecue, common, or garden vari-ety, can take on extra touches. As thus: Kill and dress quickly a fine yearling wether, in prime condition but not over-fat, sluice out with cool water, wipe dry inside and out with a soft, damp cloth, then while still hot, fill the carcass cram-full of fresh mint, the tenderer and more lush the better, close it, wrap tight in a clean cloth wrung very dry from cold salt water, then pop all into a clean, bright tin lard stand, with a tight-fitting top, put on top securely, and sink the stand head over ears in cold water – a spring if possible.

Do this around dusk and leave in water until very early morning. Build fire in trench of hard wood logs before two o'clock. Let it burn to coals – have a log fire some little way off to supply fresh coals at need. Lay a breadth of galvanized chicken-wire – large mesh – over the trench. Take out carcass – split it half down back bone, lay it flesh side down, on the wire grid, taking care coals are so evenly spread there is no scorching. After an hour begin basting with 'the sop.' It is made thus. Best butter melted, one pound, black pepper ground, quarter pound, red pepper pods, freed of stalk and cut fine to almost a paste, half a pint, strong vinegar, scant pint, brandy, peach if possible though apple or grape will answer, half a pint. Cook all together over very slow heat or in boiling water, for fifteen minutes. The sop must not scorch, but the seasoning must be cooked through it. Apply with a big soft swab made of clean old linen, but not old enough to fray and string. Baste meat constantly. Put over around four in the morning, the barbecue should be done, and well done, by a little after noon. There should be enough sop left to serve as gravy on portions after it is helped. The meat, turned once, has a fine crisped surface, and is flavored all through with the mint, and seasoning.

The proper accompaniments to barbecue are sliced cucumbers in strong vinegar, sliced tomatoes, a great plenty of salt-rising light bread – and a greater plenty of cool ripe watermelons, by way of dessert.

Pot Luck in the Ozarks
—Charles Morrow Wilson, *Gourmet*, II/5 (May 1942)

Hear first about the spareribs – how they grew to a crisp sweet goodness . . . the ingredients were about six pounds of spareribs, without too much fat, and a bottle of barbecue sauce, bought at the store some months before. Mame had cooked the ribs outdoors over a green hickory woodfire in a rock oven . . . You pick off the sweet tender meat with your fingers . . . In all my life, in all my travels through this hemisphere and part of the other, I have never eaten meat so delicious as Mame Crenshaw's hickory-smoked spareribs. A poor man's dish, certainly, but brothers and sisters, all the gold buried at Fort Knox can't buy the flavor of these spareribs.

Noodle-Barbecue
—featured recipe, advertisement for Crisco, *Good Housekeeping*, XCVI/2 (February 1933)

Practically a whole meal in itself!

NOODLES: 1 package noodles, 1 cup dry bread crumbs, 6 table-spoons Crisco.

MEAT BARBECUE: 1 small onion, chopped, ½ bay leaf, 4 tablespoons Crisco, 4 tablespoons flour, 1½ cups stock or water, ½ teaspoon salt, ½ teaspoon pepper, a few grains cayenne, ⅛ cup currant jelly, 1 tablespoon lemon juice, 1 tablespoon chopped pimiento, slices of left-over roast

Fried Noodles: Cook noodles in boiling salted water until tender. Drain, pour cold water over. Melt Crisco in frying pan. (Fry with Crisco, the vegetable fat.) Add crumbs. Fry to crispy brown. Add noodles. Warm. Mix thoroughly. Serve hot with Meat Barbecue: Brown onion, bay leaf in wholesome Crisco. Blend in flour. Slowly add liquid. Stir. When sauce thickens add seasonings. Strain. Return to heat. Add currant jelly, lemon juice, pimiento. Add slices of cold roast.

Luau in Your Own Backyard
—Trader Vic, *Gourmet*, XII/9 (September 1952)

Get as much tropical decoration into your background as possible – anything to create an illusion of Hawaii. If you can't have ukuleles and live music, use phonograph records for atmosphere. Putting your guests in the right mood is the big thing. The most important item in a to-do of this kind is the liquid refreshment and it should be tropical. I wouldn't even think of serving highballs.

Modern Recipes

Tandoori Lamb Chops
—Alexandra Zeitz

8 lamb chops
1½ cups (360 ml) yoghurt
3 tbsp lemon juice
1 tbsp vinegar
8 cloves garlic, minced
1½ inches ginger, minced
1 tbsp kosher salt or to taste
4 tbsp vegetable oil, divided
1 tbsp ground cumin
1 tbsp garam masala
1 tsp ground coriander
1 tsp ground turmeric
1 tsp chilli powder
½ tsp cayenne pepper
1 tsp paprika

Using a sharp knife, cut ¼ inch slits in each lamb chop to allow marinade to penetrate. In a large bowl, mix yogurt, lemon juice, vinegar, garlic, ginger and salt.

In 1 tbsp vegetable oil, toast spices in a small pan until aromatic but not burnt. Add to yogurt mixture and stir to incorporate. Transfer the chops to the marinade, cover and store in refrigerator overnight.

Next day, when ready to cook, remove the chops from the marinade. Let stand for 30 minutes. Cook in a tandoor (or alternately slow smoke roast) until medium or desired doneness. Serve hot with naan and tandoor-roasted vegetables.

Peri-peri Chicken
—Alexandra Zeitz

Chicken

1 2-inch piece fresh ginger, peeled, minced
1 large shallot, peeled, minced
3 garlic cloves, peeled, minced
2 cups (480 ml) packaged peri-peri sauce
½ cup (120 ml) olive oil or vegetable oil
½ cup (120 ml) fresh lemon juice
1 teaspoon kosher salt
1 teaspoon freshly ground black pepper
8 chicken thighs or one large whole chicken, quartered

Glaze

3 tbsp butter
2 garlic cloves, minced
½ cup (100 ml) *peri-peri* sauce
2 tbsp fresh lemon juice

In a large bowl, combine the ginger, shallot, garlic, peri-peri sauce, oil, lemon juice, salt, and pepper. Stir. Add the chicken to the bowl and coat with the marinade. Cover and let marinate overnight in the refrigerator.

The next day, remove the chicken from the refrigerator and let stand for 30 minutes.

For the glaze, melt the butter in a small saucepan over medium-high heat. Add the garlic and cook until it begins to brown, about 2 minutes. Add the *peri-peri* sauce and lemon juice. Reduce the heat to medium-low; simmer for 2 minutes.

Slow smoke roast until skin is golden and thermometer reads 165°F (75°C).

Once cooked, transfer to a platter. Pour the warm glaze over. Serve with salads and pap.

Coupé-coupé Sandwich
—Alexandra Zeitz

1 ¼ cups (300 ml) Maggi sauce
2 tsp cayenne
1 ½ tsp garlic powder
salt and pepper to taste
2 lbs flank steak
2 poblano peppers
1 onion
1 baguette
½ cup butter, softened

Mix together 1 cup Maggi sauce, 1 tsp cayenne, 1 tsp garlic powder, salt and pepper in a large bowl. Place the steak on a sheet tray and brush marinade heavily onto steak. Cover and place in refrigerator. Let the steak marinate for at least 1 hour, preferably overnight.

Slow smoke roast until desired doneness. Well-done is traditional.

While the meat is cooking, roast the poblano peppers until the skin is brown and blistered. Remove the skin from the peppers and slice. Peel and cut the onion vertically. Grill until slightly charred. Once the onion is cooked, slice. Slice the baguette in half, brush with olive oil and toast on the grill.

Mix together the butter with the remaining Maggi sauce, cayenne, garlic powder, salt and pepper.

When the meat is cooked, let it rest for 5–10 minutes. Slice thinly across the grain. Prepare the sandwich with the steak, peppers, onions, butter spread and baguette.

Sosaties
—Evan Fowler

1 lb (450 g) pork shoulder, diced in 1-inch cubes
4 cloves minced garlic
salt and pepper to taste

1 medium onion, finely chopped
2 tbsp oil
1 tsp ground coriander
¼ tsp ground cumin
1 tsp curry powder
1 tsp Tabasco sauce
½ tbsp brown sugar
⅓ cup (80 ml) fresh lemon juice
1 tbsp apricot jam
½ cup (120 ml) water
1 tsp flour

Toss pork with garlic and salt and pepper and let sit for a minimum of one hour, covered, in the refrigerator. Meanwhile, sauté the onions in oil until golden. Stir in the coriander, cumin and curry powder, Tabasco, brown sugar, lemon juice and jam. Add the water. Bring to a quick boil, stirring constantly.

Remove from heat. When the mixture is thoroughly cooled, pour it over the meat, then cover the bowl and refrigerate overnight or at least 12 hours. Thread meat on skewers and slow smoke roast until cooked: 145°F (63°C).

Save the marinade in which the meat was soaked. While the meat grills, transfer the marinade to a heavy pot. Bring to a boil. Spoon out a bit of the hot liquid to blend with flour. Whisk into a smooth paste and stir gradually into the pan. Pour the sauce over the meat to serve or serve alongside.

Jamaican Jerk Chicken
—Erin McGuire

3 tbsp allspice berries
2 tbsp peppercorns
1 bay leaf
½ small onion, chopped
4 scallions (spring onions), chopped
5 cloves garlic

1 small habanero chilli
3 tbsp fresh thyme
1 tbsp fresh ginger, grated
2 tsp salt
1 tbsp cider vinegar
1 tbsp brown sugar
2 tbsp vegetable oil
6 chicken legs
1 lime, cut into wedges

Toast the allspice and peppercorns in a skillet over medium-high heat until fragrant, about one minute. Process with the bay leaves in a food processor until finely ground. Add and process the onion, scallions, garlic, habanero chilli, thyme, ginger, salt, vinegar, brown sugar and oil until a paste is formed.

Coat the chicken legs and breasts under and above the skin with the paste, and refrigerate for 12–24 hours. Slow smoke roast until internal temperature reaches 165°F (75°C). Serve chicken with lime.

Barbecued Pork (*Char Siu*)
—Noah Williams

4 lb (1.8 kg) pork shoulder
½ cup (120 ml) soy sauce
¼ cup (60 ml) honey
3 tbsp oyster sauce
2 tbsp Chinese rice wine
1 tbsp five-spice powder

Trim the excess fat off of the pork shoulder. Cut the pork into lengthwise strips 1.5 inches wide and 1 inch thick. Mix all other ingredients in bowl and pour over the strips of pork. Coat well and marinate for 4 hours or overnight in refrigerator. Slow smoke roast until an internal temperature of 145°F (63°C) is reached, basting occasionally.

Chinese Roast Duck
—Noah Williams

1 7-lb (3.2-kg) duck (including head, wings,
and feet preferably)
¼ cup salt

For Coating
3 tbsp Chinese rice wine vinegar
3 tbsp honey

For the Sauce
⅓ cup (80 ml) hoisin sauce
1 tsp sesame oil
1 tsp Shao-Hsing wine or sherry
6 scallions (spring onions), white part only, cut into 2-inch
pieces, with ends sliced to make fringes

Prepare the duck. Remove all excess fat and membrane as well as
any remaining feathers, and thoroughly rinse the inside and outside
with cold running water. Pat dry. Sprinkle the outside of the duck
with salt and rub in well. Rinse the salt off. Allow the water to drain.

Slide your fingers in between the skin and meat of the duck
and separate the two, eventually working your whole hands underneath the skin. Make sure to get the legs as well. Once separated,
take a clean kitchen towel and pat the top of the meat and under-
side of the skin to remove any excess moisture.

With a knife, remove the first 2 joints of each of the wings (and
feet). Insert a chopstick under the wings and through the back to
lift them away from the body.

Holding the duck with one hand, carefully ladle a quart (560
ml) boiling water over the skin of the duck, making sure to get
under the wings and between the legs. It is preferable to do this
over the sink. The skin will darken and tighten slightly. Allow 30
minutes for skin to dry.

In a pot, bring to a boil 3 cups (675 ml) of water plus the
ingredients for the coating. Repeat the same procedure for coating

the skin. Refrigerate duck hanging overnight to allow the skin to dry out.

Mix together the ingredients for the sauce. Cover and re-frigerate until ready for use.

Slow smoke roast until an internal temperature of 165°F (75°C) is reached. Serve with sauce.

References

1 Barbecue Beginnings

1 C. K. Brain and A. Sillen, 'Evidence from the Swartkrans Cave for the Earliest Use of Fire', *Nature*, CCCXXXVI/6198 (1 December 1988), pp. 464–6.
2 Ibid.
3 Bent Sørensen, 'Energy use by Eem Neanderthals', *Journal of Archeological Science*, XXXVI/10 (October 2009), pp. 2201–5; R. E. Green et al., 'A Draft Sequence of the Neandertal Genome', *Science*, CCCXXVIII/59797 (May 2010), pp. 710–22.
4 John Gardener Wilkinson, *The Manners and Customs of the Ancient Egyptian*s (London, 1841), vol. II, p. 35. Nathan MacDonald, *What Did the Ancient Israelites Eat?* (Grand Rapids, MI, 2008), p. 32.
5 Robina Napier, *A Noble Boke off Cookry ffor a Prynce Houssolde or Any Other Estately Houssolde* (England, 1468).

2 Man and Feast

1 Elizabeth S. D. Engelhardt, 'Cavemen and Firebuilders', in *Republic of Barbecue: Stories Beyond the Brisket* (Austin, TX, 2009), p. 121.
2 *Bricriu's Feast*, translated by George Henderson, at www.yorku.ca.

3 Eric Kline Silverman, *Masculinity, Motherhood, and Mockery: Psychoanalyzing Culture and the Iatmul* (Ann Arbor, MI, 2001) p. 120; Jan Pouwer, *Gender, Ritual, and Social Formation in West Papua* (Leiden, 2010) p. 30.

4 Tony Perrottet, *The Naked Olympics: The True Story of the Ancient Games* (New York, 2004), p. 116; Thomas Keightley, *The Mythology of Ancient Greece and Italy* (London, 1838).

5 Perrottet, *The Naked Olympics*, p. 116.

6 Kaori O'Connor, 'The Hawaiian Luau: Food As Tradition, Transgression, Transformation and Travel', *Food, Culture and Society*, XI/2 (June 2008), pp. 149–72.

7 Francis Ignacio Rickard, *A Mining Journey Across the Great Andes* (London, 1863), p. 50.

8 Ibid., pp. 50–51.

9 William Dickson Boyce, *Illustrated South America: A Chicago Publisher's Travels and Investigations* (Chicago, IL, 1912), p. 388.

10 Nelson Algren, *America Eats* (Iowa City, IA, 1992), pp. 7–8.

11 George Thornton Emmons, *The Tlingit Indians* (New York, 2001), p. 140; Dan Huntley and Lisa Grace Lednicer, *Extreme Barbecue* (San Francisco, CA, 2007), p. 220.

12 S. E. Wilmer, *Theatre, Society and the Nation: Staging American Identities* (Cambridge, 2002), p. 28.

13 Louis Albert Banks, *An Oregon Boyhood* (Boston, MA, 1898), p. 146.

14 Arthur Firmin Jack, '*Chet*': Also Other Writings (New York, 1899), pp. 59–60; Jason Sheehan, 'There Is No Such Thing as Too Much Barbecue', in *This I Believe* (New York, 2007), p. 218. For a more complex discussion of the role of barbecue restaurants in the Civil Rights movement, see Jason Sokol's *There Goes My Everything* (New York, 2007).

15 Andrew Warnes, *Savage Barbecue* (Athens, GA, 2008), p. 171.

16 Richard Reinitz, 'Vernon Lewis Parrington as Historical Ironist', *Pacific Northwest Quarterly*, LXVIII/3 (July 1977), pp. 113–19.

17 Hal Rothman, *LBJ's Texas White House* (College Station, TX, 2001), p. 178.

18 Ibid., p. 179.

19 Tom Wolfe, *The Right Stuff* (New York, 1979) p. 286.

20 Charles Perry, 'The Bull's Head Breakfast in Old Los Angeles', *Cured, Fermented and Smoked Foods: Proceedings of the Oxford Symposium on Food and Cookery 2010*, pp. 242–7.

21 M.F.K Fisher, *Among Friends* (Berkeley, CA, 1970), p. 156.

22 John Grisham, *A Time to Kill* (New York, 1989), p. 141; Doug Worgul, *Thin Blue Smoke* (London, 2010), pp. 17–21.

23 John Steinbeck, *The Pastures of Heaven* (New York, 1995), pp. 137–8.

3 Poles, Holes, Racks and Ovens

1 Bob Shacochis, 'Burnt Offerings', in *Food: A Taste of the Road*, ed. Richard Sterling (San Francisco, CA, 2002), p. 54.

2 Fannie Merritt Farmer, *The Boston Cooking-School Cook Book* (Boston, MA, 1896), p. 152.

3 Edith Thomas *Mary at the Farm* (Norristown, PA, 1915), p. 273.

4 Maistre Chiquart, *Du Fait de Cuisine*, 1420 Folio 9 'The Provision of Cauldrons', trans. Terence Scully (Tempe, AZ, 2010).

5 Ibid., Folio 7, 'The Provision of Meat'.

6 James W. English, 'Hawaiian Beach Camp', *Boy's Life* (July 1949), p. 31.

7 Blanche Howard Wenner, 'The Luau (from a Tourist's Point of View)', in *Hawaiian Memories: Poems* (New York, 1910).

8 Fanny Chambers Gooch, *Face to Face with the Mexicans* (New York, 1887), p. 74.

9 Gerard Fowke, *Archeological Investigations in James and Potomac Valleys* (Washington, DC, 1824), p. 62.

10 John Morison Duncan, *Travels through Part of the United States and Canada in 1818 and 1819* (Glasgow, 1823), vol. I, pp. 297, 299.

11 Fatema Hal, *Authentic Recipes from Morocco* (Singapore, 2007), p. 86.

12 Felipe Fernández-Armesto, *Near a Thousand Tables* (New York, 2002), p. 15.

13 Michael Symons, *A History of Cooks and Cooking* (Champaign–Urbana, IL, 2000), p. 74.

14 Ibid.

15 Martha McCulloch Williams, *Dishes and Beverages of the Old South* (New York, 1913), p. 158–9.

16 Forest and Harold Von Schmidt, 'Come and Get It!', *Gourmet*, I/5 (May 1941), p. 10.

17 Hi Sibley, 'How to Construct an Outdoor Fireplace', *Popular Science*, CXXVIII/6 (June 1936), p. 105.

18 Sunset, *Sunset Barbecue Book* (San Francisco, CA, 1945).

19 Advertisement for Bar-Be-Kettle, *New Yorker* (13 November 1948), p. 92.

20 Advertisement for Cook 'n' Tools in *Gourmet*, XII/4 (April 1952), p. 30.

21 Trader Vic, 'Luau in Your Own Backyard', *Gourmet*, XII/9 (September 1952), p. 55.

22 Ellen Schmidt, 'Mr. and Mrs. Ray Burke "Make Out" on One Salary', *Corpus Christi Times*, 8 June 1951, p. 18.

23 Charles Mercer, 'What Type of Man is John Steinbeck?' *Cedar Rapids Gazette* (Iowa), 18 October 1953, p. 9.

24 Sam Sifton, 'Roasting a Pig Inside an Enigma', *New York Times*, 7 January 2004, p. F1.

25 Ibid.

4 A World of Barbecue

1 Elisabeth Rozin, *Ethnic Cuisine: The Flavor Principle Cookbook* (Lexington, MA, 1983).

2 Ed Gibbon, *The Congo Cookbook: African Recipes* (Lulu, 2008).

3 Pat Conroy, *The Prince of Tides* (New York, 1987), p. 224.

5 Competition and Connoisseurship

1 Lolis Eric Elie, *Smokestack Lightning: Adventures in the Heart of Barbecue Country* (New York, 1996).
2 David Dudley, 'Taking the Low Slow Road to Perfect Barbecue', *Baltimore Magazine* (July 2000).
3 Lolis Eric Eli, 'The Tao of Barbecue', *Forbes* (Summer 1997), pp. 125–7.
4 Dana Bowen and Josh Ozersky, 'The Pay Is Awful but Judging Barbecue Has Its Rewards', *New York Times*, 5 July 2006.
5 John Shelton Reed, *Kicking Back* (Columbia, MO, 1995), p. 153.

6 Sauces and Sides

1 William Lindsay White, 'Kansas Beef Tour', in *The Food of a Younger Land*, ed. Mark Kurlansky (New York, 2009), p. 273.
2 Elizabeth S. D. Engelhardt, *Republic of Barbecue: Stories Beyond the Brisket* (Austin, TX, 2009), p. 16.
3 White, 'Kansas Beef Tour', p. 274.
4 Zora Neale Hurston, *Dust Tracks on a Road* [*c.* 1942] (New York, 1995), p. 232.

Select Bibliography

Barbecue History and Culture

Adams, C., *The Sexual Politics of Meat: A Feminist-Vegetarian Critical Theory* (New York, 1990)

Algren, Nelson, *America Eats* (Iowa City, IA, 1992)

Bass, S. J., '"How 'Bout a Hand for the Hog": The Enduring Nature of Swine as a Cultural Symbol of the South', *Southern Culture*, 1/3 (1995)

Browne, R., *Barbecue America: A Pilgrimage in Search of America's Best Barbecue* (Alexandria, VA, 1999)

Egerton, J., *Southern Food: At Home, on the Road, in History* (New York, 1987)

Elie, L. E., *Smokestack Lightning: Adventures in the Heart of Barbecue Country* (New York, 1996)

—, 'The Tao of Barbecue', *Forbes* (Summer 1997), pp. 125–7

Engelhardt, Elizabeth S. D., *Republic of Barbecue: Stories Beyond the Brisket* (Austin, TX, 2009)

Fernández-Armesto, Felipe, *Near a Thousand Tables* (New York, 2002)

Hirsch, G., *Gather 'Round the Grill: A Year of Celebration* (New York, 1995)

Huntley, Dan, and Lisa Grace Lednicer, *Extreme Barbecue* (San Francisco, CA, 2007)

Limon, J., 'Carne, Carnales, and the Carnivalesque', in *Dancing with the Devil: Society and Cultural Poetics in Mexican-American South Texas* (Madison, WI, 1998), pp. 123–40

Linck, E. S., and J. G. Roach, *Eats: A Folk History of Texas Foods* (Fort Worth, TX, 1989)

Moss, Robert, *Barbecue: An American Institution* (Birmingham, AL, 2010)

Reed, John Shelton, *Kicking Back* (Columbia, MO, 1995)

Rozin, E., *Ethnic Cuisine: The Flavor Principle Cookbook* (New York, 1987)

Sterling, Richard, ed., *Food: A Taste of the Road* (San Francisco, CA, 2002)

Saporito, B., 'Sniffing out Barbecue', *Fortune*, CX/4 (1984), pp. 239–44

Symons, Michael, *A History of Cooks and Cooking* (Champaign, Urbana, IL, 2000)

Vateto, James, and Edward Maclin, eds, *The Slaw and the Slow Cooked: Culture and Barbecue in the Mid South* (Nashville, TN, 2012)

Warnes, Andrew, *Savage Barbecue* (Athens, GA, 2008)

Barbecue Cookery

Garner, B., *North Carolina Barbecue: Flavored by Time* (Winston-Salem, NC, 1996)

Gibbon, E., *The Congo Cookbook: African Recipes* (Lulu, 2008)

Hal, Fatema, *Authentic Recipes from Morocco* (Singapore, 2007)

Jamison, C. A., and B. Jamison, *Sublime Smoke: Bold New Flavors Inspired by the Old Art of Barbecue* (Boston, MA, 1996)

Raichlin, Steven, *Planet Barbecue* (New York, 2010)

Snider, R., *Secrets of Caveman Cooking for the Modern Caveman: Recipes for Grills and Smokers* (Phoenix, AZ, 2001)

Voltz, J., *Barbecued Ribs, Smoked Butts and Other Great Feeds* (New York, 1990)

Websites and Associations

Websites and Associations

Competition barbecue site
www.thesmokering.com

The science of barbecue
www.amazingribs.com

Advice on cooking with fire
www.firepit-and-grilling-guru.com

Directory
www.bbq-festivals.com

Blogs

All Things Barbeque
http://pelletenvy.blogspot.com

BBQ Forum
http://bbqblog.com

BBQ Blog
http://bbqguyblog.blogspot.com

BBQ Junkie
www.bbqjunkie.com

Associations

Memphis in May
www.memphisinmay.org

World Barbecue Association
www.wbqa.com

International Barbecue Cookers Association
www.ibcabbq.org

National Barbecue Association
www.nbbqa.org

Kansas City Barbecue Society
www.kcbs.us

Acknowledgements

We would like to thank Andrew Smith for the opportunity to write this book and also our families, especially Molly Deutsch and Preston Johnson, for putting up with us while we did so. We would also like to acknowledge the spirit of all who put meat and smoke together in the pursuit of excellence.

Photo Acknowledgements

The author and publishers wish to express their thanks to the below sources of illustrative material and/or permission to reproduce it. Some locations of artworks are also given below.

Photo AG/Keystone USA/Rex Features: p. 89; photo andreveen/ iStock International: p. 112; photo Facundo Arrizabalaga/Rex Features: p. 101; British Museum, London (photos © The Trustees of the British Museum): pp. 17, 20, 22, 23, 30–31, 49, 52; photo Chameleons Eye/Rex Features: p. 81; photo CSU Archives/Everett Collection/Rex Features: p. 38; Egyptian Museum, Turin: p. 18; photos Everett Collection/Rex Features: pp. 32, 63; photo Patrick Frilet/Rex Features: p. 90; photo Joe_Potato/iStock International: p. 76; photo Jorisvo/BigStockPhoto: p. 86; Library of Congress, Washington, DC: pp. 35, 36, 40–41, 43, 93; photo Mike Longhurst/ Rex Features: p. 73; photo © W. Robert Moore/National Geographic Society/Corbis: p. 92; National Museum, Brussels: p. 48; photo © Abraham Nowitz/Corbis: p. 80; photo Oddjob: p. 66; photo Dave Penman/Rex Features: p. 60; photo Sanjuro/ BigStockPhoto: p. 50; photo Etian Simanor/Robert Harding/Rex Features: p. 79; photos Sipa Press/Rex Features: pp. 96–7, 99; photo © Keren Su/Corbis: p. 77; photo Werner Forman Archive/ Egyptian Museum, Turin: p. 18.

Index